# GROUPS, GIMMICKS, AND INSTANT GURUS

# Groups, Gimmicks and Instant Gurus

## An Examination of Encounter Groups and their Distortions

**WILLIAM R. COULSON**

HARPER & ROW, PUBLISHERS
New York, Evanston, San Francisco, London

FIRST EDITION

STANDARD BOOK NUMBER: 06-0615885

LIBRARY OF CONGRESS CATALOG CARD NUMBER: 74-183639

# Acknowledgments

The philosophy of encounter groups presented in this book is a joint production. I wrote the book, but my colleagues at the Center for Studies of the Person—Bruce Meador, Douglas Land, and Carl Rogers —influenced my thinking decisively (although they won't let you hold them responsible for what I say).

My family, Jeannie and the children, contributed vitally by helping me live through the ways in which a person can change through the powerful stimulus of the encounter group, yet hang in with those who are given in his life, and they with him. I owe them everything for sticking with me.

Many people permitted me to be in their encounter groups. Some of them wrote to me later about their encounter experiences. They turn up again and again in the pages that follow. There would be no book without them.

Good friends of the Mary Reynolds Babcock Foundation helped by making a grant that carried me through a portion of the time I was working on the encounter research project recounted in Part V and doing early drafts of the book.

Special acknowledgment goes to Dr. Weldon P. Shofstall, State Superintendent of Public Instruction in Arizona. As dean of students at my undergraduate alma mater, he was my first professional mentor. I say "professional" because my first mentor was my father. But Dean Shofstall gave me my earliest firsthand example of personal involvement in one's profession, where the person doesn't submerge himself in professional style, yet where the fullness of his commitment can never be doubted, because it is obvious that his wish is to give him*self*. Dean Shofstall was the first educator I knew. I dedicate the book to him.

W.R.C.

La Jolla, California

# Contents

# PART I

# Introduction

## CHAPTER 1

# THE FREE ENCOUNTER
# VS. THE GROUP MOVEMENT

When I first got involved in encounter group work, for a few years I was very cautious about touching people.

I used to wish that we were freer with one another in my family as I grew up, but for some reason it was hard to express affection. As I got older, I didn't hug my father or kiss him, and I found it difficult even to hug my sisters. So when I got in encounter groups and people were open and spoke personally and felt close and, often, wanted to express their feelings with a touch, I was troubled. I too was feeling close to people. The feelings were wanting expression but I was tied up and shy.

Part of my problem was that I worried how it would look. Back in my family, if I were to embrace my sister after years of not doing so, I feared she might say, "What got into you?" Or even if she didn't say that, even if she said, "Wow, I really like that!" even if she said something positive, I think I would have been terribly embarrassed. I think I would have wanted to say (though, of course, I would not have said it), "Look, how about if I hugged you and we pretend I didn't?"

Another imaginary conversation, the kind that rattled through my head in encounter groups and kept me frozen to my chair, went like this:

In my imagination, I would finally take the bull by the horns, get up and cross the room to the person I felt close to (preferably someone in tears, because then I would have a better excuse: "I'm only consoling you"). But when I would reach out to this person, perhaps just to pat her shoulder, she would say, "Feeling a little sexy, are you?" And while disappearing into the floor, I would say to myself, "Yeah, maybe that's it. Maybe I'm just horny. Who knows how far I might go if I had the chance."

But when I finally got up the nerve (it took me two years), walked that last mile across the room, put my hand on that person, I found to my surprise that the sexual part of my feeling was not all that great. I slowly came to realize that physical feelings and sexual feelings are not identical, though to some extent one involves the other. And then, when I began digging through the research, I even found that animal psychologists have been able to isolate two separate needs experimentally, the need for physical contact and the need for sex. It turned out that just wanting to touch somebody didn't mean wanting to seduce them!

This is an example of something personal and important I learned because I was lucky enough to be in encounter groups. I feel freer for it. I doubt it would have happened from reading research reports alone.

An encounter group is an experiment in psychological community. It is a shared opportunity for personal learning. Typically it is a gathering of a dozen or so people with whom you gradually sense that you can try what you have wanted but not previously had the nerve to do, with whom you can talk about personal matters—such as the fear of touching. Or to whom you can speak directly, if you muster up the courage, saying, "Here is how I see you," or asking one of them to speak to you in the same way. All of this is very hard to describe, however, because then it can sound as if there might be some formula for encounter. It isn't so. Encounter is what just happens when people have enough time together that they get around to what they have always postponed in customary social settings, where expectations are more easily located. An encounter group is a pretty free place. If at the beginning someone says, "What are we to do?" the person who convened the meeting might reply,

"What would you like to do?" Then the individual is thrown back on his own resources and may begin to reveal what he usually withholds.

One can be open in an encounter group not because the participants are particularly trustworthy, for they are just people like people everywhere, but because the meeting goes on so long that it becomes clear that everyone share in the risk and therefore wouldn't want to hurt the others.

With these characteristics, of few expectations, of great freedom, and of a gradually sensed safety, encounter groups foster sharply accelerated personal growth in their participants. People change after encounter groups, in ways that they report please them greatly.

Me too. My own life has changed in valuable ways by my participation in encounter groups. In some eight years of leading such groups I have known countless others to change also. But I see encounter groups as both good and bad.

①*The good part: a chance to recover the freshness.* Encounter groups began because there didn't seem to be enough room in our highly organized society for people to meet just as people, when we weren't playing roles, when we weren't being guarded, when we weren't feeling compelled to impress one another and meet one another's expectations. Encounter groups began because we needed a place to try ourselves out, a place where performance wasn't central, where we could make mistakes and still stay together.

②*The bad part: they are becoming an institution.* The encounter attempt to recover the freshness of life is turning into a movement, with new rules of procedure, recognized centers for doing it, gurus, formulas, known truths, hierarchies in charge, and credentials for being a practitioner—to the point that something else will have to be invented to recapture the freshness. Encounter groups are losing it as they become a cultural institution themselves.

To be frank, encounter groups are now drowning in gimmickry.

## The Group Movement

You have seen in the news magazines the extremes of what goes on under the banner of "the group movement": Hot-bath growth center nudes earnestly engaged. Communal flower sniffing. Group lifts. Mass face feeling. Like . . . an X-rated summer camp.

Many in the movement think they know what people need in our culture: They need freeing up. Which is not defined as being free (for who then could name what it would mean?), but is for these groupers a set of prescribable behaviors: recapturing the sense of smell, say; or learning to express anger; or touching people without embarrassment; or becoming more graceful in body movement—that is, learning to move *your* body more as *I* have learned to move mine. Many group leaders today approach their work as if the encounter were something predictable, a namable bit of business that should occur among the participants, some preferred way time ought to be spent in encounter groups, some desired outcome to group interaction. When this happens, the conservative critics who shout that "encounter groups are a subversive plot" are right (if not to shout at least to worry), for the process becomes like brainwashing.

When encounter groups were invented, people didn't know how to act in them, and thus they were a good opportunity to try themselves out free-form, without expectations, and to achieve personal learning. Now, as if this opportunity were not enough, experts invent exercises for people to pursue in encounter groups. New expectations. Postures of freedom.

Along with this development has been the emergence of a group leader profession, with standards, qualifications, ways of objectifying success and earning reputation. Perhaps the quickest, cheapest way to become known in such a new profession is to be the inventor of techniques, for the list of possible clever group activities is endless. ("Maybe we could get people to clean one another's ears and talk about their reactions," one wag suggested. "Or pick one another's noses. . . .")

I am not just kidding. A colleague sent me a manuscript to review, a manual offering ways in which encounter groups might reform education. It is one of a number now in preparation or already published. The author presents a list of "encounter games" and develops a rationale for them. For example, to get at the "vibrations" by which people "get to know each other," he suggests "Hand Contacts Hand," in which participants are in one stroke to be carried beyond our cultural inhibitions about touching strangers to a new and freeing set of nonverbal acquaintanceship maneuvers. Members are instructed to "explore" one another and afterward to talk about what they felt as they did so. A good explorer, we are told, will bypass the issue of whether or not his partner wants to be explored, for feelings of reluctance can also provide grist for the mill when later they talk about their reactions:

> Frequently, you will find that girls do not like to be touched and might hold back, at least in the beginning. A boy in our experimental group noted that when he confronted one girl, she was almost trembling.
>
> When asked to make eye contact also, a second girl sat with her head buried in her lap and afterward questioned why she could not do the exercise. Others admitted they did it because they felt they must, and they tried to get it over as quickly as possible. Still others enjoyed it and pursued contact with force. We found these differences provided excellent discussion material. . . .
>
> Now when you switch to the left hand and then both hands together, you find the whole realm of encounter dramatically expanded. There seems to be something more meaningful in such meetings. They are new and refreshing experiences which complement the more familiar and stereotyped righthand encounters. . . .

Aside from its naïveté, its completely unfounded meaning claim ("If you think you met me in my right hand, wait till you try my left!"), this gamey, microcalisthentical approach to encounter shouts, "I KNOW WHAT IS GOOD FOR YOU!" One doesn't even have to know at whom he shouts: we all need this medicine, and if not, no matter, for then we can talk about *that* after the game. The escalation of technique has gone so far toward the impersonal that a business firm has issued a set of tape-recorded group game instructions (at $300 a copy). We are

so advanced as a technological culture that a tape recorder can tell us
how we should act in order to be free. "This is your tape recorder
speaking. Take your partner's left hand. Careful now. . . ."

A journalist was fascinated by what he'd heard about encounter
groups. He wanted to try one. He joined a "marathon," a kind of
nonstop, 'round-the-clock encounter group in which participants' psychological defenses are supposed to yield more thoroughly than in the
more leisurely paced encounter because of fatigue.

As the group started, one of the participants was asked by another
what he did for a living. He answered, "I don't think that matters here.
Call me Rumpelstiltskin, if you have to give me a name." It turned out
later he was a psychiatrist, co-leader of the group.

By the group's fifth hour, the journalist had begun to doze:

It was some time after 1 A.M. that I was jarred awake by hearing Rumpelstiltskin ask Felicia, a woman with the voluptuous but strangely asexual body of a
*Playboy* foldout, whether she would go to bed with him. His question used the
coarsest word possible.

Felicia, her face blank, answered, "I don't know what that word means."

"Come on, you know what it means," Rumpelstiltskin said, goading her.

"I've seen it on walls but I *don't* know what it means," insisted Felicia. "I
was brought up very religiously."

"Take a guess, then."

Felicia suggested a very unconventional form of coupling that took me aback
even more.

"No," Rumpelstiltskin corrected her, "it means sexual intercourse."

"Well, I've never slept with a man," protested Felicia in a small voice.

"Anyway, let's hear you say the word. Go ahead, say it," insisted Rumpelstiltskin.

Felicia said it in an emotionless voice and added several other four-letter
expletives. "What's so great about that?"

"You've got a real mothering hang-up, Felicia," continued Rumpelstiltskin.
"You use it to hide your fear of offending people. You wear it like I wear this
sweater which identifies me as Bob, the Great White Therapist." (Although this
was the first admission we'd had from Rumpelstiltskin that he was the psychiatrist, none of us was surprised.) "Now," he went on, "I want you to go around
the room and say the nastiest thing you can think of to every person here.

. . . And every time you hesitate or fail to say something nasty enough, you've got to get down on your knees and crawl across the room, and kiss my hand."
Felicia turned to Rod, the Irish type, and said, "I think you're a pompous ass."
"Fine," said Bob, "but you looked back to me for support. Come on. Crawl."
We all watched, spellbound. Slowly, Felicia sank down beside Bob's chair.
"You're no better than your husband," she said to Louisa.
"My God, your life is a mess," she said to the painter's wife, Bonnie.
"I'll bet you really use women," she said to me.
Though ashen, Felicia managed to say something rude to all eighteen people in the group, but three times she looked back at Bob, and three times he made her crawl across the room and kiss his hand.[1]

If it sounds cruel, it is supposed to be for the person's own good. Of himself Rumpelstiltskin might say, "You think it's easy for me to be a mean bastard? I'll tell you, it costs me." Of Felicia he might say her sweetness was a cover-up for the hostility lurking beneath, unexpressed and therefore unexamined, a barrier to her emergence as a genuine person. Although Felicia resisted at first the crudeness in the suggestion that she change her behavior—"Do it! Now!"—she might have agreed later that the psychiatrist was right about her and meant well. When the journalist checked with Felicia a week afterward, in fact, she said it had been a growth experience, one she would like to repeat. "Me, I'm not so sure," the journalist said.

Yes, Virginia, there actually are such "encounter groups," though I hope no one I love ever finds himself in one. What if he didn't resent that kind of treatment? What if, like Felicia, he actually was grateful? What would he have learned? "Thank God for the Doctor. How could I ever be myself if not for him?"

A recent article from the *Los Angeles Times*: "She Sues over Judo in Sensitivity Course":

The sensitivity session recommended to C. G. by her employers . . . advertised that it would "increase . . . self-understanding . . . interpersonal effectiveness

1. James Halpin, "Get Down and Crawl," *Seattle Magazine*, December 1967, pp. 26–27.

. . . confidence and ability to work in group situations."

So Miss G. went. . . .

Toward the end of the course, Miss G. and one of her classmates, S. P., were encouraged "to physically demonstrate aggression and hostility."

According to . . . Miss G.'s lawyer, what resulted was a judo hold that sent Miss G. to the hardwood floor of the sensitivity training room flat on her back.

Miss G. has filed a lawsuit for $500,000. . . .

She didn't have to do it if she didn't want, did she? That's right. Unlike the bad example with which I began, the gimmicky manual for educational reform, most group exercises have an "option out" clause. The $300 tape recording, for example, cautions the group to respect the wishes of any member not to participate. "No one should be forced to do any exercise of which he is shy."

But it is hard to pull that off, not to participate when everyone else seems to be doing so easily. A person who had enough strength to say No when everyone else was saying Yes wouldn't need an encounter group. He could start his own program.

Even when the group doesn't push gimmicks, sometimes there can be subtle, compelling pressures nonetheless. Loring Woodman reports:

We got onto the subject of sex in our group, and I was explaining some of my frustration at being caught between what I actually felt and the cultural norms, between a kind of honest approach and the strange feeling that somehow I ought to be living up to a different cultural model, a model I had partly incorporated into myself but which yet was still somehow alien to the way I usually react.

In trying to bring this discussion down to the "here-and-now," as it were, I think I got talked into saying something about my feelings toward one of the girls in the group which was not really me. What started out as a general, personal attraction to this girl came out instead, under the "guidance" of the group, as a straight "I want to screw you" type approach. On looking back at this now, I feel as though I'd been conned into saying this when it was not an adequate representation of how I felt toward her. . . . Somehow, at the time, I didn't think this episode had made much difference to me—but the amount of time I spent thinking about it afterwards belies that thought. It seemed like the group had "gotten what it wanted" and was now ready to move on to someone else.[2]

Encounter groups distort what they are good at, which is a chance for a person to try himself out and make his own value discoveries, when they attempt to teach values, as in Loring's group: "You should say what you feel. Say it with directness. No need to hide here what would embarrass you elsewhere." Under that kind of pressure, a person might say, and sometimes do, considerably more than he means. And that is backward when it happens, for encounter groups, as originally constituted, were one of the few cultural occasions in which the individual had the leisure and the feel-freeness to work on the difficult process of knowing and expressing his personal, private meanings.

## The Extremity Of The Movement

On the extreme of the encounter movement is the tricky approach, as exemplified by the growth center nude: "If you take your clothes off, we will have more to talk about." This, and other group gimmicks, are called "generating data," as if the fact that each of us has been trying to live his life wouldn't give us enough to talk about.

The problem with the gimmicks is not that they are magic devices, which, if one submits, will steal one's spirit from him. No. The individual will not allow his hard-won personal style to be altered against his will; it is not easy to achieve personal change even when one *wants* to. What is bad about the extreme approaches to encounter is that they waste the time in which members could be making their own discoveries if there were freedom in the group. There is a kind of accelerated personal learning that can go on only in community, when learning reciprocates and everybody is open to surprise, even the leader. People

2. C. L. Woodman, *Perspectives in Self-Awareness: Essays on Human Problems* (Columbus, Ohio: Charles E. Merrill, in press).

just cannot achieve this kind of learning, the kind that can carry into life, the kind about values, without intimate contact with their fellows. Nobody learns in a vacuum. Hence the encounter group. But it can't be done quickly either, or when somebody is directing it, presenting a common catalog of maneuvers, prescribing psychological patent medicine, one elixer for all that ails the human spirit.

Personal learning is always stimulated within a community; to learn, one needs colleagues. But the learning is never to be laid out in advance; it is always one's own, private learning.

The only assuredly honest and lasting human learnings are these individual learnings—secret learnings, if you will—learnings stimulated within the community but that the individual speaks to no one save himself. The possibilities of dishonesty and of self-coercion are very great when *group* learning is emphasized, as has come to pass in the encounter movement. For me, the encounter group was a chance to get away from such learnings, from organization and performance, and finally to be with people, just to be myself.

"There is a view of life," Søren Kierkegaard said a century ago, "which conceives that where the crowd is, there also is the truth. . . .":

There is another view of life which conceives that wherever there is a crowd there is untruth, so that . . . even if every individual, each for himself in private, were to be in possession of the truth, yet in case they were all to get together in a crowd—a crowd to which any sort of decisive significance is attributed, a voting, noisy, audible crowd—untruth would at once be in evidence.

. . . if there were an assemblage even of only ten—and if they should put the truth to the ballot, that is to say, if the assemblage should be regarded as the authority, if it is the crowd which turns the scale—then there is untruth.[3]

We need all the power of occasion we can muster, it seems to me, in which individuals can seek their truth for themselves, for the collective's lack of success in finding it has been notable. It is too bad that

3. Søren Kierkegaard, "The Individual," in *The Point of View for My Work as An Author* (New York: Harper & Row, 1962), p. 110.

"the collective" has become a political catchword because, shouting the word in massed voices of warning, the conservatives empty it of meaning. But it is a useful word in this consideration of encounter groups.

In his own day, Kierkegaard spoke of the distinction between the individual person and man-as-specimen, and he rued the "modern notion . . . that to be a man is to belong to a race endowed with reason, so that the race or species is higher than the individual, which is to say that there are no more individuals but only specimens."[4] I think it is concern about being turned into specimens that motivates the alarm of many conservative critics of encounter groups; and I am with them, not in alarm, but in regret that the better opportunity to attain true manhood in community is being missed as the encounter movement gathers momentum, as people exhibit themselves now as types of repeatable group learnings.

The particular potency of the encounter group lies in its being an occasion for the individual to know himself better, to be able to decide for himself about himself; no expert is able to direct him as well as he can himself upon entering community with his fellows. At its best, the encounter group is thus a benign anarchy, where if participants accrue similar learnings it is only because it turns out that way, never because it can be arranged in advance. All the learnings of encounter are private, individual ones, to which the group has no claim whatsoever.

Encounter groups offend as dreadfully as any political collective, yet more immediately, when they roll along on the energy of a crowd, when they call on the individual to perform, when they become a court that decides about him and claims right of access to his secret heart.

When that happens, I want no part of them.

4. Ibid., p. 111.

## CHAPTER 2

# ENCOUNTER GROUPS AND SHOW BUSINESS

MEMORANDUM[1]
TO: Dr. William Short, Technos Institute
FROM: Your Guardian Angel
RE: Your Performance on the Sonny Johnson Show

Bill, I've been watching your television appearances (caught you on "Playboy After Dark") and have wanted to write about an uneasiness I feel; I was unable to nail down this uneasiness, however, until I saw you on the Johnson Show.

I can appreciate that you will want to get all the media exposure you can in selling the book. (By the way, I thought Johnson gave you excellent coverage, much better than he did the fellow with the dancing dogs.)

I think I worry, Bill, about what your work might do to *you*. It's going

---

1. This memorandum was delivered to me by mistake, the wrong Bill—W.R.C.

to take me a few pages to explain, and I won't want immediately to be thought critical, so please bear with me.

Let's recap what happened on the show:

Johnson introduced you as the author of *The Applied Mechanics of Human Feeling.* Well and good.

Then he said, "What do you do, Doctor?" and you answered something like, "I work with encounter groups, but maybe it would be best to show you. Can you help me demonstrate?" (I assume this was worked out with him in advance.)

With his distinctive little two-stepping shuffle, Johnson hopped up, rubbed his hands, smirked, and said, "Ready, Doctor."

So you got him and his guest to face one another, a girl named Bibi, whose last name I didn't catch. I think she was an actress.

No—first you did that thing where you lift Johnson up on your back: back-to-back you lock your arms in his, bend over, and raise him easily off his feet. I didn't get what that was for, but it seemed innocuous enough, for while you were risking nothing, neither was he—as when the exercise girl comes on some nights and has him do calisthentics with her, or in the old days of the "Steve Allen Show" when they'd stake Allen to the stage and let loose a bunch of ants. Good fun. At least not spiritually enervating.

Then you got Bibi to face Johnson. And this began the part I didn't like—not for her, not for Johnson, and not for you, my charge.

You asked Johnson to say something to Bibi.

"Pardon me, Doctor?"

"Say something to Bibi about how you see her."

"Well," he said, turning to the girl and looking a little embarrassed, "I notice that you smile all the time."

And then—we should not be surprised, should we, Bill, you and I, knowing how fragile people feel?—Bibi looked as if she was ready to cry. No act. She looked scared to death.

And I forget what she said. Something about that's just how she was made: "I've always been happy. Ever since I was a child. I smile."

Perhaps sensing disaster (I mean, what are you going to do if she cries, right on the network? you got time to give first aid?), you shifted the assignment then. You took the heat off.

So you suggested that you and Johnson feel one another's faces. "Expanding our ordinary means of contact. Using a neglected sensory mode."

And that was the "show." Literally.

"So, what of it?" you're going to ask me because you think I'm mad at you and I am.

This: I just think it's not right ("won't work," if you prefer) to put people on the spot like that.

See, the thing is that Johnson was accurately perceptive about Bibi. She did smile all the time. She giggled. Everything she said, in fact, she laughed. It was annoying as hell, and probably nobody before had ever done her the favor of telling her. But it was no favor to tell her like that, not on command.

What if Johnson had given himself his own command rather than taking yours? I think that would have been better, because he would have taken her defenses into account (for "her defenses" you can read "his own reticence," because they will mesh exactly in a social setting, his reticence and her defenses). He would have been very hesitant to tell her something honest about herself straight out, I should think. But as it was, you suggested he do it, so he went ahead. He wasn't responsible. ("Listen, Bibi, I wouldn't have said that if it wasn't to help the Doctor's demonstration.") And you weren't responsible. ("Don't do what I suggest unless you want to . . . but it wouldn't surprise me if you might want to.") Somebody almost got torn up in public *and nobody was responsible.*

So, then, okay, a TV show isn't an encounter group, and you can try some things on TV which don't work there but would be effective in a group. And if you had left it entirely up to Johnson what he should do, he might never do anything different than what already fits his style. Bibi could go on giggling, everybody dismissing her for it, nobody ever telling her, everybody still isolated. And you can help them break that up, Doctor, because there are some very effective techniques.

But where the hell were you? Did you see what happened to the girl?

You might very well know that underneath that giggling façade there's a genuine person. But I'll bet she doesn't know it! Take away her façade, *she* thinks, and there might be nothing there. No person. You might know better, but what good is that? She doesn't know *you*. You're just the commander. You're just the string-puller.

I mean, I'm only guessing about Bibi, but we'll never know, because you didn't get involved. The gimmick didn't work, and you didn't talk about *that*. (Right! Does the surgeon admit to the patient that his knife slipped? Not if he's a smart, dues-paid, guild surgeon!) You had somebody jerking away another human being's personal style. You had people taking huge risks in which you didn't share. Poor Bibi thought it was she alone who was being exposed. And poor Johnson, as soon as he saw the beginning of her tears, knew he had put his foot in his mouth. And the Doctor says, "Yes, well, let's try another one."

So you tried another one. Thank God you had sense to be in this one yourself. Johnson felt your face, but you had to feel his face, too. If he had been a patient, it would have been easy: "The old face-feeling trick. Done it a thousand times." But here you looked bothered. This was a famous face and thus, I should think, something of an unknown for you, not a face you could quickly absorb into the doctoring system. A face at last with the capacity to throw you. In front of a million eyes, with Sonny Johnson's famous face as object, you couldn't face-feel with aplomb, could you? You and the patient finally were on a par. You suffered too. You were thrown off balance with him. You couldn't be calm, couldn't abstract yourself, couldn't simply "understand the dynamics," couldn't doctor the problem away, for it was your problem too. Thank God, I say.

You know how much trouble I have with the concept of doctoring, when it comes to human souls. I cringe when I see people yielding their individual judgment to you in the apparent belief that you must know better or how could you be called Doctor? (And, Bill, for you too I cringe, because I hate to see them leave you out of it. I mean, who will help you get well if you have to be doctor? Another doctor? Is there an infinite regress of doctors?)

You may or may not have good clinical judgment, but that's not the issue here. The issue is that any doctor position is false when what we deal with is problems of spiritual, human relational growth. Now, people are quite capable of believing that doctors exist. You can foster that belief—or, humanely, you can let them see who you are.

Relationships are qualitatively different when someone is allowed to doctor, standing outside those relationships and calling them like a square dance leader. Risks are different when one takes them under instructions rather than finding his own. When a doctor stands by, calling the action, whatever change follows for the individual because of his participation is not something that he will own later. He can excuse himself, for he acts on command, not on choice. Which is not to say that there isn't sometimes plenty of courage needed for an individual to undertake the routines you suggest. But it's a kind of solo courage, rather than a relational confidence; a lonely making courage, the courage to allow oneself to be the fool while everyone else looks on. There was plenty of risk for Bibi in the exercise you gave her, and for Johnson too, but it was the kind of risk that, once taken, could only lead to isolation. It was not a risk produced between them; it was a risk you suggested for them. And thus, even if it had not aborted, the experience of speaking openly to another person wouldn't have been something that belonged to them later. As it was, that it was a *routine*, was highlighted by its abortive nature. They performed, embarrassingly, in front of those million eyes—and we can only hope that as time passes they will forget it happened.

If I may say so, Bill, my earlier analogy between your work and that of a surgeon is apt, because both surgery and your human potentials psychology are forms of treatment under which the patient immediately suffers, albeit for his own alleged benefit. Surgery aside, it strikes me that if the patient must suffer from psychological treatment, it is truer to the condition of our inherent connectedness as human beings that the doctor overtly share in the suffering.

In the face-touching demonstration, you did suffer. One could see it. And although Johnson said, as tentatively he touched your face, "Am

I doing it right, Doctor?" it was obvious that your answer could only be (though I don't recall that it was), "Right now I don't know any more about this than you do."

"Am I doing this right, Doctor?" The question reveals a patient's typical understanding of the nature of psychological treatment: The doctor stands outside the struggle his treatment suggestions promote. Sometimes, I suspect, the patient *mis*understands, for, in fact, the doctor suffers also (as you did, apparently, in the face touching). But often, in appearance and in fact, for whatever high ethical and scientific motives, you do stand outside.

Don't you see that from the position outside *you have a completely unreliable perspective on the patient's dilemma?*

The dilemma? "Dare I be foolish or not." Panic. Confusion.

Who would allow himself willingly to be foolish, on a stage empty of other fools? So the patient looks for assurance: "Am I doing this right, Doctor?"

Existentially, the doctor cannot resist having an opinion, because, standing outside the issue posed to the participants by the exercise, standing ouside the confusion that is real for them now and will be in the future, he has an objectivity that makes him "know" what is happening, that makes it possible for him to render an opinion (or knowledgeably to dodge one: "It would not be good for you if I answered that") —an objectivity that of course any good doctor knows is absolutely unimportant, but the patient doesn't know it.

Can you see that the situation is different when the doctor becomes a participant? Then the answer to "Is this right, Doctor?" can be neither opinion nor dodge but has to be something like "How should I know? I'm a human being, too." Then, at that moment, if the patient believes the doctor, there is no more patient, no more doctor, just persons *(just persons!)*—humble, damaged, potent as hell to invent healthy lives when help reciprocates between them. Anything else is counterfeit.

I have been scolding you, Bill, and I shouldn't, of course. Let me end this memo on an upbeat. I talked to Martin Buber the other day. He and I are becoming friends. He said, listen!—"Every living situation has, like a newborn child, a new face, that has never been before and will never come again. It demands of you a reaction which cannot be prepared beforehand. It demands nothing of what is past. It demands presence, responsibility; it demands you."

Yeah, man. Presence. It won't come in a kit.

# PART II
# The Encounter Event

CHAPTER 3:

# WE DON'T KNOW WHAT
# TO DO WITH OUR FEELINGS

For a long time I didn't know what feelings were. "Listen for the client's feelings," my supervisors would say when I was training to be a psychotherapist. But I didn't know what they meant.

I was afraid to admit this, for it seemed the other students understood. So I read a lot of books about counseling theory. They explained that the content of a therapy client's expression was one matter: the words he said. But the feeling tone could very well be another: for example that he was nervous in saying his words. If I responded only to the content —"You're saying that you never have dated girls"—there would be no therapeutic progress; the client would remain stuck in his superficial self-description; he might as well have spoken to a tape recorder. But if I reflected to him the feelings—"It seems to really bother you, about the dating"—then we would be deeper inside his experience and making progress toward getting beyond what blocked him. That, at any rate, is what I learned in the books.

But it was very hard for me to realize that in practice. I was reluctant to embarrass the other person by grasping and reflecting to him anything other than the obvious in what he said. And the obvious, of course, was the content. What I know now is that both my *reluctance* and the client's anticipated *embarrassment* were feelings and that therapy would have occurred even if we had talked only of these matters. But they were *between us* and at the time I believed therapy was only about *him*.

I was able to see that the theory actually worked only when, with more experience, I found that it didn't hurt the person for me to grab onto his part that he ordinarily hid, this feeling part, and that it didn't hurt me either. It brought us closer, of course, and there was whatever danger we cared to make in that; but the point is that it wasn't a violation of the client for me to hear the feelings in what he was saying; in fact, he welcomed it. For example, if someone were letting a small edge of sadness show and I said, "You're a little sad about what you are saying, aren't you," and then he started to cry: well, it turned out neither of us had to apologize for the revelation; it was neither awful that he cried nor awful that I had a part in it.[1]

How different that is from life, where when a person is crying, we try to pretend he isn't. We all look away and make up a conversation until he has composed himself.

How did it get that way, our reluctance to honor inner experience? I think it has something to do with the performance orientations we acquire early in life and that our school and work relations conspire to

---

1. This example can reveal a useful distinction between feeling and emotion. *Feeling* is a kind of uncertainty or hunch or inner embarrassment that is ordinarily reserved but can be spoken of in a caring relationship. And it is in finally saying what has thus been reserved that one may get emotional. Feeling is an inner mumbling, a demiconversation that longs to be open between the speaker and his hearer. Its definition is thus an operational one.

But emotion is to be defined *physiologically;* it is the uncontrolled spilling over, the physiological agitation hat may come when something too long withheld is finally expressed. It is not the same as feeling.

In saying that feelings and emotions are not the same, I am not so much interested in making an *in re* distinction as in pointing out how these terms are used in relationships. Thus "You never talk about your feelings" doesn't mean "You never cry or laugh—do it for us now" but means "You seem always self-contained. You don't yield. You talk only about what you are sure of." In sum, "You don't allow yourself to be vulnerable."

Feelings are to be defined by what you do with them—offer them or withhold them —and that is why they are an important influence on the quality of a relationship and why they are so often the focus in encounter groups.

maintain. I think it has to do with our lack of conviction that being ourselves is good enough to get by on.

If we have indeed learned to distance ourselves from our feelings, I think it is primarily in our institutions that it has happened, prototypically in our schools. I want to show how schools teach that feelings are to be hidden; how they teach that to be a student is to be knowledgeable, not ignorant; and how, in doing this, they have turned upside down their founding purpose and have made quite likely the invention of the encounter group; for encounter groups fill the learning niche schools have abandoned.

## The Missing Element At School

One way of looking at school is to say it is a place where one learns to speak: to manipulate verbal symbols, to work with the spoken and written word. One learns to talk in schools. Unfortunately, the schools have shied away from one of the most important areas of speech: the area of things that are difficult to talk about. The missing element in schools is concern with teaching people to talk about things that are difficult to say.

What are these difficult things? By and large they are the feelings: the things that are hard to explain because they are not well-formed concepts. They cannot be written on blackboards, for the words haven't yet taken sufficient form that we can write them. Of feelings one doesn't know quite what needs to be said. If one is to speak at all, it will be stumblingly. These are the things of which one says inside when feeling cautious, "I'd better not say this." When he is not just cautious but is down on himself, he says, "I *shouldn't* feel this way." (I will give some examples soon.) They are not just the feelings, though; they are also half-formed ideas. Sometimes they are barely conscious things. Always they are potentially creative. Were they to be heard, they would supply everybody with new information.

One way of defining a school is to say that it is a place which puts a high premium on saying things well. Students and teachers value looking good to one another and among themselves. Look good! Say smart things! Approval and evaluation, of teachers and of students, is very important in school. What the whole evaluation system is about is *appearance:* "Above all, look good!"

When "look good" is that important, people go into hiding. Evaluation then affects not just the classroom but carries over to all the relationships of the school. People learn very quickly in schools only to show those sides of themselves that are guaranteed approval. With good friends they might risk more; but with teachers, students, colleagues, and supervisors they rarely go beyond it. Creativity suffers.

## What Could Be Done About It?

People could sit down to talk with one another on regular occasions when there is not a topic to discuss. They would then do doing what we now call an encounter group.

A better name for an encounter group is a person group. Most groups in our culture are functional groups in which we relate to one another as functions: the teacher function to the student function, parent function to child function, pastor function to parishioner function. Rarely do we schedule opportunities to relate to one another in groups just as persons. Most often when we arrange a meeting we must have a topic to discuss, an agenda to meet, and roles to fulfill. But in the encounter group there is no discussion topic. One relates person to person, as impoverished as that might seem in prospect and as rich as it can be in the experiencing.

Another way to define it is by remembering how I defined a school: a school is a place that puts a high premium on saying things well. On this dimension, an encounter group is the opposite of a school. It is a place in which it comes to feel safe to say the things that can never be said well, a place in which one comes to feel that it is okay to say things rather badly if necessary.

## Things That Can Never Be Said Well

Here are some examples of "things that can never be said well": Once when we were doing an encounter workshop for a school and because there were sixteen hours ahead in which we didn't have a topic to discuss, one man turned to another, with whom he had been teaching for years, and said with a sigh, "Well, I really didn't want to say this, but I guess I might as well: You never have been an easy person to like!"

That's the kind of thing that can't be said very well. It can't be said well, because it is not entirely up to you then what happens next, and those things not entirely in your own control can never be said exactly smoothly. Having said something negative like that to someone, you now owe him something: you owe it to him to hear him, to confront with him the hurt that now he surely will feel. You owe it to him not to run away, to see it through with him. You owe it to him to hear what now he will say in reply, and you owe him a response to that in turn. *Negative feelings* can't be said well. They have to be said badly. We usually hem and haw when saying them. And they turn out to be very *involving*. A good motto is: Don't say such feelings if you want to remain aloof.

At the other end of the spectrum of feelings are the positive ones. They too are hard to say. A colleague told me:

When first we were married, I think my wife and I were afraid to let on how deeply we felt our love, though I am sure each of us hoped the other would guess. This must have been so, because we found ourselves developing a kind of litany, a sing-song chain of "I love yous," in which the sheer quantity of words was to make up for an inability to express the quality of the feeling. Behind this quantitative approach to the expression of our love was the fear that if we let the other know how deeply we loved, we might get hurt. In my own head— I later learned she was doing the same in hers—I projected the possibility of the following exchange, which was enough to keep me quiet about my feeling:

I would say, "You know, I really do love you very deeply."

And she would reply, "That's interesting." Or, "I see." Or, "Turn on the TV," or anything less revealing than my own admission.

It is as hard to talk about the deeply positive feelings as it is about the negative feelings, for saying feelings of either sort makes one vulnerable. It is this characteristic that, though it makes feelings hard to say, also gives them their potential for knitting us together with those with whom we are finally able to share them.

That expressing feelings makes one vulnerable can be seen from the very nature of the examples I have given. For safety's sake we usually limit ourselves—surprisingly, even in important relationships—to saying the kind of things to which we can predict the response. That is why so much of social communication is in fact meaningless. Things don't need to get said, because we already know what they are. But with feeling, with something deeply true, one cannot predict the response; it will *matter* what the other person says. That is where the fear comes from in thinking about saying it.

It is feelings that, unexpressed, keep us apart, that emphasize the differences we think there are between us, that keep us from knowing we are similar in rather touching ways. It is isolating to have feelings that one isn't sure others have. The isolation will not be breached by reassurance: "Oh, everybody feels that way." But in hearing others' feelings, in hearing the personal, specific part of their feelings, the part that rarely is talked about; in getting a firm grasp on the feelings of these other, specific people with whom one shares, the isolation can be breached. Nothing less seems to work.

Expressed, feelings have the potential of getting us together, because, expressed, they make sense of what was shadowy and guessed at before. The man in the school workshop who was told he was difficult to like could have guessed how people felt though he didn't want to hear it any more than they wanted to say it. But as long as he had to guess and couldn't talk about it, there was no resolution. It was only when what was felt was finally said that there was any hope of changing things.

I do not wish to oversimplify and say that all that must be done to get people together is to start expressing feelings. No. Feelings are indefensible, and one doesn't want indiscriminately to abandon his defenses.

Feelings are literally indefensible because they are deeper and more complicated than reasons. Therefore they cannot be explained in terms of reasons. There is no argument with which to defend them. There is thus high risk in saying one's true feelings.

Feelings *seem* indefensible because, as psychologists would say, often we are taught as youngsters, "Don't feel that way" (it doesn't matter what—just don't feel it). Feeling for many of us is *out*.

Finally, feelings are indefensible because if you say them you just might drive people away. I said before that feelings expressed have the potential of getting us together with people; but if feelings are hard to say at first, they are also hard to hear, and it may be that if you try to say them, people will not want to listen. They just might leave. If getting left is an elemental disaster, then feelings are indefensible.

If there is to be room for the indefensible in life, as I think there must be if we are to get beyond loneliness and to grow, a special occasion is necessary, the kind of special occasion in which people are unlikely to leave quickly. *An encounter group is simply such a special occasion.*

CHAPTER 4:

# INSIDE AN ENCOUNTER GROUP[1]

One popular format for encounter groups is the weekend workshop. In the case of the group that is the focus of this chapter, the group met a few hours on a Friday night, again Saturday morning, in a third session Saturday night, a fourth Sunday morning, and in a concluding session Sunday afternoon.

Ten people formed the group. Two of them were there as "facilitators," group leader–psychologists Carl Rogers and Richard Farson. The other eight, strangers to one another, were there because they were willing to participate in a first-time experimental filming of an encounter group. They represented a wide variety of social categories: a divorced woman, a schoolteacher, a seminarian, a business executive, WASPs, a Black, a Eurasian woman. Although they were handpicked for this wide range of social characteristics, the group members were not selected for problems or for personality type. They were not especially gifted or

1. The initial descriptive material in this chapter is based on the transcript of a sixteen-hour weekend encounter group arranged by W. H. McGaw, Jr., of the Western Behavioral Sciences Institute and the Center for Studies of the Person, and depicted in the Academy Award–winning documentary film "Journey into Self" (McGaw–WBSI, 1968). The film is available through Psychological Cinema Register and the Western Behavioral Sciences Institute, La Jolla, California. Used with permission.

especially troubled. This group can thus be taken to be fairly representative of the kind of group that might gather for a weekend encounter. Only one of the members had had previous encounter experience.

## The Beginning

The group began with this (verbatim) statement by Carl Rogers, the only structuring it was given:

I'm glad we all had a chance to have dinner together because it gives a little chance to get acquainted, at least a few of us; but I feel as though really, we really are strangers to each other in spite of that—with lots of geographical distance and occupational distance, and everything. And, I feel like saying just one or two things to start with, from my point of view. One is that this is our group. We really can make of it anything we want to make of it, and for myself, I don't have any prediction, except that by the time we end Sunday afternoon, we'll probably know each other a lot better than we do right now; but how we may want to go about it, or what we want to do, that's really up to us. And I think that it is an opportunity to *be* in the group as fully as we can; maybe in some respects to try ways of being or ways of relating to each other that we never quite have had nerve enough to try before, where in ordinary life situations it seems like it's too impossible. In a sense, it's an opportunity to try out new ways of behaving with other people; there's that in it too: things that we have sort of wished we might be or do with others and never have quite had the nerve —maybe we will have the nerve here. I don't know, but at any rate from here on in, as far as I'm concerned, it's up to us. . . . Oh yes, one thing I did want to say: I feel a lot of anticipation about this group; I really look forward to getting to know you. And at the same time, I'm apprehensive; and I don't think it has much to do with the lights and the cameras. I think I'm always a little apprehensive in not knowing what a given group is going to be like. I don't know who we are, how we're going to get along, whether anything is going to come of this. So I feel a very double feeling: I feel excited and full of anticipation; I feel a little on the scared side, too.

After such a nondirective introduction, the group usually searches for something to talk about.

Often in the early going it will manage to come up with something like a topic, something the members can move cautiously around. This group settled for a time on the subject of marriage. The facilitators simply let it develop. They neither encouraged the discussion nor impeded it, but, as one will do when there seems to be a topic under discussion in a social group, they joined in as participants themselves. It was a safe discussion, for members could speak generally about the topic. They could be spared risk. The risk of saying what can only be said without caution—*the feelings*—will come only later and gradually as the degree of safety in the group is sensed.

There are ways to speed up this gradual passage of time. For example, some encounter group leaders urge that the group members talk only about feelings, or talk only in the here-and-now. One structured exercise some leaders use to move a group more quickly is the "secret pool," in which each individual writes down anonymously on a card a secret about himself, something that typically he would hide from others; these cards are then passed in and the leader reads them off. But this group was a free group. There were no rules, no games.

Jerry, one of the members of the group, is a middle-aged businessman, successful in his field, by his own description seen as easy to get along with, friendly in a hale-fellow way but not close to people, not really easy to know other than superficially.

Jerry participates easily in the topical discussion of the first few hours of the encounter group, in which people are confining themselves to saying things halfway, not being insincere but thinking that's all they mean, remaining all the while a safe distance from how it feels inside.

## The First Hour

In the first hour of his group, Jerry drops this comment into the discussion:

We have tremendous fears of insecurity and many times these same things which you are so insecure about you look back weeks, months, even years, and what you were insecure about—thank heavens, you cannot remember, and you would like to, at least in my case, I would like to get an honest feeling about myself period, and act this way in all cases. This is where the thing gets off the track because you keep thinking about what other people are expecting of you and if you feel you are under a pressure-type thing when you are going to act one way to meet this what you think is the way of doing it. In other words, many times this happens in marriage: "How should I act as a husband?" Many times I may not feel like acting this way, but I act this way in certain cases and this is a false thing and probably my wife does sense this is not me and probably this is some of the problem in dealing with everybody. But I know this is a complicated thing and we cannot really set up any great decisions about it, but in a group such as this it seems I have been noticing it is a difficult thing to open up and you wonder why. Why are we like this and why are we reluctant to open up?

Jerry's statement makes little sense when written out. But it is the normal stuff of social conversation, and ordinarily, in social discourse, we pretend to understand it, nod agreement, and add our own comment, quite possibly not related to his at all—but it doesn't matter, for we don't hope for much in social discourse.

What Jerry says would need a translator to be understood. And one will notice as the group goes on that translation becomes less necessary. Later, Jerry begins to speak not from what he guesses will be acceptable but from his experience; as he does so, we can check what he says directly against our own experience and either see a difference from ourselves or identify with what he expresses. Less translation is necessary as Jerry later comes to say what inside himself he really means.

His intentions are good enough in this early going. He moves toward the personal, he speaks from time to time of I, but then he darts quickly back to the general, confining himself mostly to generalizations about how it is with *people,* knowing the worst he might then get is an intellectual argument about his observation, but that he is not likely to have someone try to lift his cover and say, "May I come in?" In the defensive orientation that most of us, like Jerry, bring to new situations, to speak generally seems safest.

## The Fifth Hour

Jerry gets a little closer to what he means in the fifth hour of the group:

As far as people are concerned I . . . I, in a sense like being around people, but I . . . I only like to go up to a certain point, then; from there I don't like to get too close to people, and it's because of . . . uh . . . well, it's whenever you're in things like this, you really can't explain yourself because I suppose we don't really analyze ourselves, and it's very difficult . . . uh . . . it's complicated, but, for example, if I got to know you, Keith . . . uh . . . there would be a certain point that I wouldn't want to, at least the way I feel now, that I wouldn't want to get to know you too well, and . . . when you say, "Well, why do you feel like this?" . . . I . . . I can't say. Maybe it's because I don't want to be bothered, and yet it may be because as Beth says that . . . uh . . . you get up to a certain point and . . . I feel if you get to know me too well, you'll reject me, I guess. Maybe that's what I'm thinking about. I don't know. If other people really know us, they might find things about us that . . . uh . . . they don't like."

He is beginning to speak for himself and of himself. But his "me" still shifts back to the general "us" at critical moments.

## The Eighth Hour

The eighth hour has Jerry in the personal; though still describing himself, he is *present* now to what he says. Finally it is clear of whom he speaks:

I look at myself with strangeness because I have no friends, for example, and I don't seem to require any friends.
VOICE: Here?
JERRY: Any place. I really mean friends. I have not one friend. I don't seem to need any. Yet in my own area I'm fairly well liked I assume, at least I haven't found anything different than that. This is a shocking thing, because I feel I'm all wrong and that I do need people. Yet at this point I don't seem to need any of you.
ROZ: How can you not need people?

JERRY: Well, as I say, I feel that's the wrong thing, but I'm trying to be honest at this point. I don't know if I am honest even in saying it, but it's the way I feel not only in this group but in any area. And it's a mystery, because people seem to need other people; not "seem to" but they *do*. And yet I can't seem to realize this or . . . or . . . really *feel* it, rather, is what I'm saying.

CARL ROGERS: Is there a . . . you say you have not a single friend. Is there no one you feel close to or whom you feel you would let come close to you?

JERRY: Well, my . . . uh . . . my parents. (Pause.) Outside of my wife, of course, but that's a different relationship. If you mean somebody that I would have to confide in and felt that I just *had* to do it. . . .

ROZ: That you *wanted* to do it. . . .

JERRY: Beg your pardon?

ROZ: That you wanted . . .

JERRY: That I wanted to?

ROZ: Rather than . . . rather than . . . than *had* to.

ROGERS: I think he's saying, at least the way I understand it, he said, "If I was desperate, maybe I would go to my parents." But I think Roz is asking, "Isn't there anybody you'd like to share yourself with?"

JERRY: (pauses and slowly shakes his head) No.

## The Eleventh Hour

In the eleventh hour, Beth, the group member who was about to have her twenty-fifth wedding anniversary, is speaking of her relationship with her husband, of how their marriage was so much less rich than she had hoped:

BETH: I used to blame him for everything that was wrong in our marriage, but I've quit doing that, because I realize that it wasn't all him—that it was me. Now I blame me, and I think it's all my fault now. I've changed to the opposite side of the fence. . . . Because I can't give real love and I can't give it back to him. That's why I have to give my affections to the cat. I've told him so and he knows it, but he still loves me anyway, which is wonderful.

ROZ: I don't believe you believe he loves you, and I don't believe you believe it's wonderful.

BETH: Well—I admire him for being able to stick with me.

As Beth talked, and cried, Rogers noticed that Jerry seemed to be touched by what she was saying:

ROGERS: Without knowing it she must be talking to you, Jerry.
JERRY: Well, I am pretty choked up. I wouldn't be able to say much.

Beth continued to speak, members of the group speaking with her. Jerry's distress was obviously growing. His chin trembled and he stared at his shoes, hands clasped tightly in front of him. Roz, the young Eurasian woman, was across the circle of ten chairs, where she could see Jerry directly. As his agitation grew her own did too. Finally Roz got up, walked across the room, and put her arms around Jerry. He began to cry.

Jerry wept for a long time. Roz held him. She cried too. The other members looked on and seemed touched.

ROZ: (crying) All along I really felt he didn't feel deeply about anything. We accused him of that last night.
BETH: He hasn't been able to express his feelings . . .

The group sat in silence and then Jerry left the circle, going off to compose himself before returning. After a bit, Rogers left to be with him. Then Rogers returned. While Jerry was gone, Keith, one of the other members of the group, related Beth's discussion to his own marriage. When Jerry returned Keith was talking. The group paused. Eyes turned to Jerry. Jerry looked at them a moment, evidently in thanks, lit a cigarette, and then the group went on with Keith.

## Why Did Jerry Cry?

Jerry had remarked that what he wanted to say was complicated. He said this in the first hour and again in the fifth. It wasn't complicated at all: He wanted to cry. But the opposite is true, also: It was *so very complicated* that the only way it could be expressed was in tears.

Jerry never said why he cried, and no one in the group asked him. One might guess that Beth's comments set off feelings in Jerry about his own marriage, that he wept because of problems there. But I think, more deeply, Jerry's tears might have been for us all: That he wept because it is at times a painful thing to try to live one's life.

He wept, too, I should think, because he finally came to feel what he had said earlier about not having any friends. One can make such a statement and keep a distance from it, or one can feel the deep hurt of knowing that indeed he has not one friend.

Complicated and mixed up and painful as it felt for Jerry to try to see himself in this way, all that was needed to uncomplicate it happened in that moment: Roz came over to Jerry, she held him, and Jerry cried. Jerry sobbed like a baby and Roz just cradled him.

## The Sixteenth Hour

In the sixteenth and final hour Jerry told what the eleventh hour's encounter meant to him:

Well, the first thing I think of is that it is possible to have other people, to have other people who can reach out if you in turn will reach out to them. I mean, it is possible for this to happen; and it's a feeling of becoming closer to people, especially to individuals. It seems that what I am saying is more from a textbook. I don't know why I struggle with it so much. The only thing I can relate is this feeling that happened with me regarding Beth's problem—and then the response from Roz immediately seemed to take me back into the group or back into the human race, I guess you'd say —that isn't a good term, but back into other people's feelings. They're concerned. They *are* concerned. They can be. People can be concerned about you regardless of what type of individual you are. This realization has come to me. It's things that you have read about, but I couldn't possibly say that this would ever happen to me no matter if we sat here for a month. I could never picture some person being concerned over me. They could listen to my story and maybe say a few remarks like, "I'm sad for you," or "I'm sorry for you." That's what I'd say I'd take out of the meeting—that there is a tremendous potential or possibility of this happening—not just here but any place that I try to have it happen.

From his cautious garble of the first hour, Jerry has progressed in the course of his sixteen-hour encounter with nine strangers to a touching summary of a deep truth in his life: "People can be concerned; but I never would have thought someone could be concerned over *me*, no matter if we sat here for a month."

It's so hard to ask for concern (we fear no one will want to give it), so hard, too, to offer it to someone with any directness (we fear that it may not be our concern that is wanted but someone else's). Yes, we all speak easily of concern *in general*, but concern given generally is worth nothing where we live. "Could any of you be concerned over me?"— the possibility of an inadequate response is so frightening that we hesitate to ask the question.

If the question is hard to ask, it is also hard to answer, a least believably. Anyone who risks asking for something personal is not going to be easily reassured just by words. Roz had to get up and move for Jerry. She had to run the risk of walking what must have seemed a very long way, across the room, to Jerry. "This is *I*, Roz, walking to *you*, Jerry." Only then could Jerry experience that people were concerned. "It's true! Someone is concerned over *me!*"

That it takes a lot of time and safety to be able to ask for something personal, that it takes a lot of time and safety to be able to move for someone, that our hurried and institutional lives have little of either time or safety—these are some of the reasons encounter groups have become popular.

## The Individual And The Group

I look back over my selection of material from sixteen hours of transcript and note that it does not focus on interactions between group members. That is because I do not think the interactions are essential in themselves, only in what they allow. They allow for the passage of time in the enclosure of the group, for the assurance that slowly can develop between the members that "It's okay"; one is not rejected when his routines have run out; it is possible for people to stay together after all. Only in striking instances like Jerry's, amounting I am sure to no more than a sixteenth of the time spent in this effective encounter group, are people able to say what they mean. Freeze an encounter group at any one point and what is said will seem more or less phony. But it doesn't matter, for the critical group event is simply the process of time passing and the group's staying together. Within this process every now and then, not very often but often enough that one doesn't forget it, the *singular* event occurs: A bit of richness shines forth from a person.

Even in encounter groups, people seldom manage moving exchanges, impressive levels of dialogue. The moments of drama in encounter groups, such as Roz's embrace of Jerry and Jerry's tears, are usually nonverbal. And in themselvse they are unimportant: If something real is exchanged in such a dramatic moment, it comes as the result of an inner happening, as a sign.

Sometimes because of others' efforts to be more honest with themselves and to say the honest thing, a striking statement or action can be called out of a person. But *he* says it. It belongs to him, not us, and we can only cherish him for it. Rarely is it part of a verbal exchange. The things that people say *to* one another or propose to do *with* one another in basic encounter groups are often off the mark, just as they are on social occasions—they try to say helpful things and that's not really very helpful, or they think they've got to reach over to pat the person who's in distress. About these statements and propositions there is often an element of contrivance, even in encounter groups (and now, as encounter groups become popular and people know what typically happens in them, "even in encounter groups" can become "especially in encounter groups"). But eventually it doesn't matter if people miss the mark in their overt gestures toward one another. Eventually, with the passage of time, the people in encounter groups come to know that they are regarded for themselves. Words become unnecessary. With the passage of time, the group members can sit in silence for one another; or they can say words, with both speaker and hearer knowing that though the words may miss the mark, a loving intention exists nonetheless. And then, with this kind of acceptance, a person gradually can come to say or show *what he means*. There is nothing to do then but to love him for it.

It's so rare! Where else do people say what they mean? Where else do they sit still with one another long enough?

## CHAPTER 5:

# THE NECESSARY AND SUFFICIENT CONDITION FOR ENCOUNTER

The necessary and sufficient condition for an encounter group is that there be an *occasion* for it. The characteristic of this occasion is one of extended time, for given the unstructured approach I am advocating (and, indeed, which I think provides the only possibility for genuine encounter), time is needed for people to come to express what ordinarily they are afraid of, their feelings.

The total quality of this occasion is its unstructuredness, its lack of requirements, even the requirement of being a "good group member" as this is coming to be understood in the canons of the encounter movement. If you give people some idea of what is expected of them, typically they will do it.

The occasion, this sole necessary and sufficient condition of the encounter, is one of stopping the action long enough for people really to come to see one another, for them gradually to have with one another the things which may be so simple, that ordinarily they are too embarrassed to mention them.

Some research organized a number of years ago by Richard Farson, one of the facilitators of Jerry's group, indicates that people cannot manage this; that, as a matter of fact, they cannot manage to encounter one another if they are simply thrown together for a lengthy period of time. This is because, without having experienced encounter before, they are unable to assume permission to talk differently than in ordinary social discourse. Without previous encounter experience, or without the permission-giving presence of the designated facilitator, people placed in a free-form group setting will simply while away the time chitchatting, vying for leadership, or in other ways avoiding honest expression. But put a facilitator in the room, imply that he knows what he's doing, and then suggest to him that he not do anything except to be himself as he can manage, then this assignment of leadership seems both to prevent people from wasting time in such social manuevers as contending over leadership themselves and to give them sufficient permission to speak honestly.

People need an excuse at first to speak honestly, and the mere presence a titled outsider can be sufficient excuse—he doesn't have to do anything special.

Thus, one characteristic of the sole necessary and sufficient condition of an encounter group is that this occasion-that-becomes-encounter has implicit within it the permission to be different than our ordinary selves. You saw how Carl Rogers gave this permission overtly in his opening remarks to the filmed encounter group. People are so shy of appearing different that they will not risk the kind of personal expression that comes to characterize a good encounter group without first knowing that it is permitted. Rogers's brief remarks warrant their risk. The personal example of the facilitator taking his own gentle risks can also warrant it.

The leader of an encounter group errs if he tries to *make* the group happen. He errs in missing the opportunity to find out what people are like when they are not being manipulated. He errs in taking away from the members the rare opportunity to be what they want to be, without performance expectations. He errs also because *it simply isn't necessary* to manufacture the events of encounter. I am quite convinced that there is something in each of us that longs to be personal even if ordinarily we don't dare it. If this is what we want, then it will come out in time if there is a sufficiently uncluttered occasion with other people. But if this is what we also are afraid of, then it will indeed need that time to come out. It has to be the kind of time in which there is not some other task toward which we could gravitate, for though each of us wants to be open, we will seize whatever communal excuse there is to avoid it; if someone gives us a topic to discuss, we shall gladly do that, for when there is a topic there is some standard of excellence that can guide our performance (we have all been to school); but who will know what excellence is when it comes to expressing *himself?*

A person's feelings lie closer to his self than do whatever impressive topical comments he can contrive. If there is to be room for feelings in our communal lives, an uncluttered special occasion is necessary. And this is all that is necessary.

The encounter will happen, then, if you give people sufficient time together without a distracting task and put someone with them as leader who will not do traditional leaderly things—who knows enough not to get people organized, not to tell them "how to encounter," not to set an agenda or get motions passed, and, most assuredly, not to put them through tricks, for they will do them!

It can work this way: Since the facilitator doesn't do leaderly things, the group members flounder about trying to find something to say that will please everybody; this proves boring in time, and, eventually, because the leader doesn't rectify the situation, someone expresses his honest frustration. Feelings have now been expressed, and immediately the situation is no longer boring. Boredom is defined as a condition in which people's attention is scattered, in which there is nothing present worth all of us attending to together. But, as you can imagine, if someone were to say, "Frankly, I am bored," then we would all suddenly be attending to the same event. I mean, that's the sort of thing that gets attention—not if it's offered as attention-getting, but if it's said honestly. It gets our attention either because it is what we were feeling too or because someone finally took a risk. The encounter then begins. The exchange of feeling is so naturally compelling that the encounter proceeds and deepens on its own energy.

## Another Group

The discussion of the sole condition of encounter will be more concrete if it can be rooted again inside an encounter group. Let's go into
another group then, this time through the eyes of David C. Davis, whose
experience wasn't as positive as Jerry's. Davis, a graduate student participating in his second encounter group as part of a course requirement,
describes the experience:

To begin with, I was trepidatious about the second weekend. I had had a very
meaningful experience the first weekend; but I had talked to many people who
had had negative experiences, so I was less than enthusiastic about what might
happen. The negative experiences were mostly as a result of what I think of as
"group games-playing."

This included the [encounter] buffs, who, without any of Fritz Perls's insights
or ability, try to emulate what they have misunderstood as his technique. They
pounce on some poor, hapless member of the group and without themselves ever
hearing or seeing, proceed to try to provoke an emotional breakdown.

Another type is the person who has learned a few words of "group" and goes
around shouting "you're intellectualizing!" "only the here-and-now!" and other
such slogans.

Fortunately, my reservations were unneeded. My group not only did not have
any . . . buffs, but we intellectualized and reminisced whenever we felt the need,
and no one shouted any slogans. We also never got around to making any rules,
which seemed to me a fine thing.

I learned several interesting things over the weekend:

1) I learned that facilitators often have as many problems as other members of
the group. We spent a great deal of our time with the facilitators, each of whom
had his own things he was working out, and one of them spent a great deal of
time reminiscing. At times I felt that this really slowed the group down, and
I got impatient, but then I reminded myself that a) she was also a member of
the group, and b) if she needed to reminisce that was what she was going to get
a chance to do.

2) I found that for some reason I didn't feel a real part of the group. This may
be because the group never did get down to being real people—though a couple
of members did, I think.

I know that the slowness of the group was partly due to my not being able to present myself—so to speak. The previous week a supercilious and unwarranted attack on me (so I felt) blew my cool and I lashed out spectacularly at one of the other members. This seemed to clear the air, pulled me into the open, and started us interacting.

Interestingly, each time that previous group came together at least one person would remark that someone must be missing. Because of our increasingly strong group feeling it seemed each time that there were fewer of us—that the group seemed to become smaller. As we grew closer to the people emotionally, it seemed that we also grew closer physically. This sensation did not occur in the second group.

3) I think I might almost say that I learned more about myself *after* the second weekend than during it. At least I became conscious of many things afterward. a) I realized, as one of the facilitators remarked to me afterward, that no one else could pull me into the group. I had to do it myself. b) I felt cheated (in a way) because I hadn't been able to become a part of the group—in my own feelings, that is—and was especially disappointed Sunday afternoon when I felt I had made a breakthrough and was ready to interact and there was no more group. Like everyone else had picked up his marbles and gone home just when I had learned to play. c) One thing which rankled was sitting in the court afterward, watching people, especially priests and nuns, embracing in the freest manner while I, in effect, still had my arms chained to my sides. It was depressing to discover that even nuns and priests were freer than I was.

I felt at the end of the weekend like I haven't felt for years—that everyone had found the bluebird but me.

On the way home, when my wife began to tell about a freeing experience one of the members of her group had, I almost broke down. Then, when we were sitting eating lunch, talking about the weekend, it just seemed like too much. I broke down and sobbed—for my poor self, for my inability to communicate, for all the powerful and good things that people can do for each other—and to make up for the tears I should have shed a couple of times in the group and didn't.

## Vicarious Experience

There are two contrasts with Jerry's story in Dave Davis' account that are worth drawing out. One concerns the possibility of vicarious experience: Dave was disappointed in himself because he did not risk in the second group as he did in the first. But still important personal learning was possible for him. His learning did not depend on his level of activity.

I participated in encounter groups for two years before I ever let on that I was present as other than an interested observer. The groups were not bad groups for my withholding my own participation, for others did participate themselves. I benefited both from seeing their realness and from comparing it with my own excessive shyness, a process that caused me eventually to participate more actively. Not everyone has to share equally in the encounter at the time for there to be an encounter experience for everyone.

## The Question Of Drama

As we have seen from Dave's statement, not all instances of encounter learning are as dramatic as Jerry's. Often no overt change develops for the person within the sessions themselves, but almost inevitably, if they get to the level of shared feelings, the sessions cause people to learn through reflection between times or afterward, as they did for Dave. There doesn't have to be heavy emotion for there to be encounter.

I want to lay it down again that feelings are not really the same as emotions, though often we use the words interchangeably. I am defining feelings as "the things that are hard to say," and it is in finally saying them that one often gets emotional. An encounter group is feelingful, but it is not always emotional. There are no requirements for an encounter group. How could there be? How could human engagement have a standard format?

Well, if you would turn it into a show. . . .

# PART III
# Distortions

## CHAPTER 6

# WORDS AND DEEDS

Encounter games are very powerful. Sometimes participation in one can cause a person's body to get so far beyond his head that he can't take responsibility for what happens.

## Rodney Meets The Earth Mother

One of my colleagues at the Center for Studies of the Person loaned me the following account of his experience with a group gimmick:

Belinda French and I were co-workers at the old Western Behavioral Sciences Institute, the organization out of which the Center grew. She was part of the research group which, on a federal grant, developed the expensive tape recording for self-directed groups. One day, some of us got together to try on ourselves an early version of the tape. We were a weekly luncheon group of Institute staff members and local psychologists and psychiatrists, all professionally concerned with issues in the practice of psychotherapy and in the new group methods being developed.

The twenty of us split into two smaller groups and turned on the tape recorder. "Of course I can't see who you are," the voice said, "but I want you to know that I care about you. . . ."

The tape recorder cares! Reassured, we stretched out on the floor as the recorder next instructed.

"I am going to play some music, and I want each of you to have a fantasy while you listen. Let your imaginations go. Let your mental pictures flow with the music. Don't censor. Let the music take you where it will. Afterward, to the extent that you feel free to do so, share your fantasies with the other members of the group. You will have ten minutes of sharing time. I will let you know when the time is up."

The music was Debussy. Everybody saw sea gulls. No mind. The sharing was the best part anyway. I began to know the members of the group in a new way. Apparently, the fantasy exercise had given us an excuse to show hidden sides of ourselves, sides that stayed under wraps in the more predictable weekly discussion of psychotherapy issues.

Ten minutes of blank tape was reeling itself out, and then the voice said, "Stop."

Boo! Hiss! We had just gotten started. But the tape was unrelenting.

"Stand up, please, and regroup your circle. Now, one at a time, go around the circle to each group member. Touch each person as you come to him, look in his eyes, and tell him what you feel about him."

Oh, wow. This part was frightening. I didn't know what I would say to each person. I didn't want to work it out in advance—feelings aren't what you rehearse, I said—but I didn't want to be speechless, either, when my turn came. The touching part bothered me, too. I'd be nervous, I knew. I wanted to do it right—not touching too much (don't want to look like a fairy), yet not seeming too afraid of touching (don't want to look like a *latent* fairy, either).

Phil Kane was first on my route when the group finger pointed to me. He is a psychiatrist. He and I had recently made a deal where I would do some of my therapy work out of his clinic. I put my hand on his shoulder. I trembled as I spoke, but it helped when I saw that he also was scared. "Phil," I said, "I'm really looking forward to working with you." Period.

(So I'm home safe with Phil. Actually, this is easy. Why am I shaking?)

Who's next on my route? BELINDA!

But I felt comfortable with Belinda. It was her Earth Mother style. She was very nice. And she had a way of making it easy for people to relate to her. She went out of her way for you, but easy.

I hadn't done my part before with Belinda, hadn't thanked her for being nice to me, hadn't even told her that I liked her. So I didn't just touch her arm and say, "Thank you, Belinda, I like you." Instead—this is me?—I put my arms clear around her, pulled her close, and said, "Belinda, I REALLY like you!"

I didn't see Belinda for the next three months. I mean, I saw her but usually I saw her before she saw me. I was able to hide.

Why did I hide? I don't know. I was embarrassed, really embarrassed. Then one day, Belinda caught me when I wasn't looking. "Rodney, have you and I been avoiding each other?"

"Who, me?"

But I confessed. As best we could figure out, I had scared myself. I had said more than could properly belong to me after the exercise. I didn't take time or make opportunity to clear it up with her. While it was true that I liked her, even really liked her (but probably not REALLY liked her, not two full arms worth for sure—nobody but my wife gets that!), I didn't want her to misunderstand: "Look, Belinda, I didn't mean that I love you." But I hadn't been sure that clearing it up would be anything other than defensive.

You can say that I worry too much—why can't Rodney just let things be?—but that's who I am. I worry, that's what I'm like. Possibly, deep down buried, I liked Belinda as much as I said in the game. But it's not where our relationship was, not the everyday relationship. I listened to the damned tape recorder and got unreeled.

My relationship with Belinda got worse because we were in a game which was supposed to make it better.

For personal growth to be solid, the body and the head have to grow in tandem. A game can give permission for one to do what he might have longed to do but could not take responsibility for, having not yet decided the issue himself. It can rush his body beyond his head, his behavior beyond his person. If the game thus provides too powerful a stimulus, the participant may later find himself needing to disown abruptly what he made happen under the special rules of the game. This was the case with Rodney.

This problem, of being able to take subsequent responsibility for one's behavior, is not so great in the free-form encounter as in the structured exercise, for in the free group, typically, the individual gives himself his own permissions, silently, and paces his growth trials in accord with his own assessment of his readiness and his need to retain his defenses, an assessment that can only be well made organismically, from *inside* his experience. No impersonal game, let alone another individual, can make such an assessment for him.

## On Group Norms And Freedom Of Choice

Loring Woodman comments:

One of the things that has been occupying my mind since this last weekend is the thought that perhaps what really happened in our group is that everyone (or at least the most active members, possibly including myself) had gotten onto the "encounter group kick"—that they were all playing at being "good group members," and that they had taken the game so to heart that they had considerable personal stake in their performance; so that what should have been a permission-granting experience, an it's-okay-to-be-where-you-are approach, became instead an arena in which to perform, with certain very definite restrictive norms or ground rules. These norms had grown out of initially facilitative modes of interaction, but because they had become norms, they had become exaggerated and prescriptive, and that was the end of real personal freedom in the group. I didn't understand this at the time, but I'm beginning to wonder now if that isn't what really happened to make my experience unpleasant.

In the days which followed this experience, it occurred to me that there are definite modes of interaction which are facilitative in encounter groups. Under normal circumstances these modes would evolve naturally in time out of the encounter situation; in our group, filled as it was with people who had been in encounter groups before and with a facilitator (I now think) who felt overly responsible to make the thing "go," there developed instead a perverse, exaggerated and prescriptive version of these usually facilitative norms.[1]

At best, in a gamey group, you succeed in trading one set of general norms, society's, for another and more particular set, the group's. It seems to me there is more freedom on the side of the more general.

A group game can work to effect immediate change in its players precisely because it provides such a sharply limited special occasion. The game can be over within minutes; who should not be willing to throw himself into a alternative personal style so briefly?

But, to be effective, even within the sharp time limits, all parties to

1. C. L. Woodman, *Perspectives in Self-Awareness: Essays on Human Problems* (Columbus, Ohio: Charles E. Merrill, in press).

the exercise must accept the rules. That is why the games have so little cultural utility beyond the doors of the group room.

Once I was allowed to visit a self-directed college student encounter group. I walked in just in time to hear one young man, explaining earlier actions, say to another: "I wanted to get to know you, that's why I suggested the backrub."

Extraordinary! Getting to know somebody through rubbing his back —the opposite, it seemed to me, of how things usually are. Ordinarily, in daily life, if one wants to touch someone, it is to express a closeness that he feels already. First you get to know somebody, then you feel close to him, then you even might want to express it physically.

But according to what the students had learned earlier in a "microlab" (a smorgasbord presentation of nonverbal group exercises), the everyday process could be reversed and lack of acquaintanceship bypassed. First you could touch a total stranger, *then*, because of the touch, feel close to him, then maybe even want to talk. As though the militant could go up to the street-corner cop and say, "Hold still, man, I'm going to touch you. We'll get along better."

Thus the student's remark, "I wanted to get to know you, that's why I suggested the backrub."

If only one's berubbed would hold still!

## The Toucher And The Touched

A group leader who specialized in teen-aged groups was known by young people along the circuit as "Old Touchy-Feelie-Pushy-Pokey." He carried his freed-up physical style like an aura around his body. The teen-agers knew his physicality had little to do with them. It operated indiscriminately. When he touched you it didn't mean he knew who you were. It must have been lonely for him. "Look out, here comes Old Touchy-Feelie-Pushy-Pokey."

Given the growing popularity of encounter groups and games, there are surely many people now who can say they have been assaulted by a group toucher. Sad it is that touch, which in our culture could imply the existence of an affection between people that is real and risky, which might take account of the individual uniqueness of both toucher and touched (and therefore would not touch quickly, because it respects an initial unknownness), sad it is that this possibility for confirmation between persons has been appropriated as a gamer's self-display rather than as the knowing implication of a betweenness.

This indiscriminateness of touch is sad for the recipient, for it implies the denial of his hope that what it is to be himself will not turn out to be interchangeable with what it is to be anyone else. It implies the denial of what I think each of us hopes for: That "somewhere, someday, someone will listen carefully enough to me that he notices who I am; this revelation may surprise him but he will not disbelieve it . . . and he will not quickly go away." *Then* one might be willing to be touched. In celebration.

The game-based touching is saddest, I think, for the toucher, for he misses the thrill of presence, which is only to be *found* between persons, never to be placed there. Once we saw a woman on the video tape replay of an encounter group—"Miss Kleenex" the group leader called her. From the distance of playback you could see so clearly what she did: When anyone cried, when anyone was within a mile of crying, Miss Kleenex was there, patting, rubbing, clucking—and pushing tissues. There was no room for anyone else to offer consolation in that group, for Miss Kleenex had captured the concession. But, worse, there was no room for *her*, either, for she had so stylized her participation that all she could hope for was to leech off someone else's distress. The consolation she offered, which wanted to be human, unfortunately had everything to do with her and nothing to do with the recipient—and therefore nothing to do with her, either, not really, not as a person, only as a mechanism unable to run its own risks of contact.

The CBS–TV documentary film on encounter groups, "Circle of Love," was made at the Western Behavioral Sciences Institute when the self-directed group tape was being developed. A neighbor of ours saw the film and reported herself sickened: "The tape told participants to express their feelings to one another, but not in words. My skin crawled when I saw one older man put his arms around a young girl whom it turned out I knew. I wanted to vomit."

We all know what it is to want to hug someone, and if the man in the film, with the anguish of personal, self-chosen risk, had been able to engage with the girl herself, then it might have been something pleasing. A human base for affectionate expression might have been established. But instead it came over as mechanical, at the best lecherous. Cued by a voice from an electronic box, a man and a girl, strangers, embraced. Science had synthesized I–Thou.

The woman who reported her impressions of the show had also been in an encounter group herself. She told me, "I have always had this feeling of discomfort when asked to do some of the group things. I mean, I do want to be more affectionate with people, but there has to be some base between me and this particular person before it can be human. There has to be some acknowledgment between us that this is real, and that my need to be loving dovetails with his need to be loved."

Prior to such acknowledgment, without time spent in working it out, gradually gaining knowledge of one another, there can only be blind guesswork, a mechanical forcing of one person on the other, in which both will be diminished.

"When you touch me—does it mean me? Does it mean you?" These questions will be unanswered by the group exercise. It is likely, in fact, that the answer is "No. I don't even know who you are."

## The Plenum Of Presence

To see whom we are with, in this moment, in this place; to stop for now the frantic pace of daily activity and daily deciding, to be silent if necessary, to look around and to notice who is here—this is the powerful plenum in which the encounter group operates, the here and the now. This is where persons become present to one another.

Can you render a plenum by a pea? Apparently so, for the gimmicists have succeeded in trivializing the here-and-now: "For the next twenty minutes," group leaders have been known to say, "let us have a rule that we will speak only in the here-and-now, no references allowed to the outside world." And silence: "For the next twenty minutes, let's have no words; if you want to communicate, do so nonverbally." Even presence: "Please begin each statement in the next twenty minutes with 'I.' No 'you' statements or 'they' but only 'I.' " And so those human events that could happen, and in the happening would need no verbal introduction at all, being our own discovery, now are announced to us as by the copyright holder.

Here-and-now games, nonverbal games, "I"-statement games—none of the group games even live up to their own aim. They are not here-and-now nor are they nonverbal nor are they "I" intended. Each of them requires a setting of scene and definition of rules that is verbally announced, that is directed at the group, that is dragged in from the announcer's past group experience.

## The Discovered And The Contrived

I am not opposed to the nonverbal. But it seems to me valuable enough that we could risk discovering it between us rather than having to bring it in by regulation. With all the encounter games, it is the need to contrive them that bothers me. And it bothers me because doing the gimmicks of encounter takes up the precious little time we have together, in which the genuine article might be found.

So little faith! Cannot one believe that what has been valuable to him in the past will come again if he will wait, if he will pay attention to the moment? And if it does not come under attentive circumstances that perhaps he should be getting on with his life?

Gimmicks are not necessary. The encounter can happen without them. So it bothers me when groupers haul them in. When a gimmick is going, one can't differentiate between what the gimmick makes happen and what *we* are able to achieve among ourselves.

I mean, wouldn't it be nice to learn that you and the people you find yourself with can cook up creative lives between you? That you don't have to thumb through a psychological recipe book to know what to do next?

## CHAPTER 7:

# I THROW DOWN JACK MURPHY

I didn't really throw him down, however. I put him down—gently. But the thing is, I *wanted* to throw him down.

A hundred of us were participating in a microlab at the La Jolla Program. One assignment was to find a partner for some nonverbal exercises. Jack Murphy and I got together.

Ready?

"Don't talk," the public address system announced. "Nonverbally work out a way of placing your partner on the floor. Perhaps he will want to resist and you might want to get him down vigorously. Or maybe you will find a more gentle way between you. It will be a good problem. First you put him down, and then he puts you down."

Oh, the room was suddenly filled with violence. It looked like everybody was wrestling. (We had a lot of priests in the program that summer. All that suppressed hostility. "Secretly, I will pretend this fellow is my bishop.") Grunt. Push. Trip. Grab. It looked like fun. I turned to seize Jack.

Jack cheated then. He talked. He said (these were not his words, the whole thing is exaggerated in my memory): "I am glad we are not like these others. I've known you as a gentle person. I am a pacifist too."

58

So Jack Murphy got set down gently that day, as though Ginger Rogers dipped to the floor in the arms of Fred Astaire. And the same fate was mine when Jack's turn came to aggress.

"Oh ho! See what you can learn in these games?" the group exercise advocate says. "*You* learned you were a goddamn liar."

"But I could have *told* you that!"

The next time I was in a microlab, I was determined it would be different. My partner was Larry Carlin. Funny thing, he and I had just been talking about violence.

"I have a problem with violence," Larry had said. "I'm really afraid I will get hurt."

("Ah," I thought. "I'll kill two birds. Larry must learn there is nothing to fear. And this time I will not let my actions tell lies.")

"Go!" said the p.a. system.

I grabbed Larry. He resisted. I twisted. (I had been weight lifting since the last microlab.)

I'm winning. Larry is going down. Our problems are being solved.

CRRRACKKK!

Larry's ankle broke.

It was beautiful then. Realization of what had occurred filtered through the hall. Someone started to sing. Spontaneously, voices were raised: "For he's a jolly good fellow, for he's a jolly good fellow. . . ." Larry grimaced through the pain, raised up on one elbow and waved. He was a hero.

I tried my best to recover my balance too. I showed leadership. I found a doctor, and when the campus police came with the stretcher to haul Larry away—"What is this? Why are they on the floor? Why are they all singing?"—I spoke for the group, "It's kind of like physical education, officer."

It may be that I am so strongly opposed to gimmicks in encounter groups because I think I might be too violent. I do know that I love competition. I really like games, when they are recreational. We have something at home called "Fight of the Week," where all the children attack me and I attack them. A glob of strugglers on the floor. Our mother says it's too violent, but I love it. All that grabbing. All that beating on one another. Sometimes there's blood. I'm glad I have a family.

Another thing that has made it personally hard for me to think of leading group games is that I have had the fantasy of saying, "All right, let's all get up and make a circle in the middle of the room. . . ." And then I get up in the middle of the room, and I look around, and nobody has joined me. They're still sitting on the sides. They're looking at me. Some are chuckling. . . .

## CHAPTER 8

# "IN THE BEGINNING, THERE WAS PATHOLOGY . . ."

Seeing the potency and popularity of encounter, which had its early development outside the medical tradition, psychiatrists have now begun to be involved with it. And that is a good thing, because it will make them better people. But it will be an unfortunate development if, once involved, the more insecure among the doctors try to control its spread, limiting "the practice of encounter groups" to their own profession and taking the appropriate medical stance—that, like life itself, the groups are very dangerous.

"Dangers in Group Therapy Told by Two Psychiatrists . . . If Practitioners are Unskilled," a recent newspaper headline announces, except they don't mean just group therapy but, the article reports, "sensitivity training, marathon encounter and nude encounter therapy." The various group activities are mixed up in people's minds, and rightly so, because the differences between them are not so important as the fact that all of them are forms of restorative human communication. Here is the revealing way the article begins: "Group psychotherapy is a powerful tool that can do serious and permanent damage in the hands of unprofessional and untrained therapists, two psychiatrists said Wednesday . . . at the National Conference of the American Group Psychotherapy Association."

These articles never begin, "Group psychotherapy is a powerful tool *which can do serious and permanent good. . . ,"* though at least as much good is done as damage. But psychiatrists are paid to be expert about damage, and apparently they see its possibility everywhere.

You should know that in a way I am in competition with psychiatrists and have some interest in putting them down. The competition comes in the form of the La Jolla Program, which I mentioned in passing in the last chapter.

The La Jolla Program began in 1967 as a summer training program for campus ministers, many of whom felt themselves to be without an important function on their college campuses. Intensive exposure to encounter groups, we believed, might help them perform an important function indeed upon return to their own campuses. They might then be among the few people in their institutions who would believe that good things could happen from listening to others and who would be willing to let themselves be seen as persons. That couldn't be a bad influence, we felt, if American institutional life suffered as much from impersonality as people said.

The program has grown in size and scope. Participants now include a cross section of institutional life, no longer just campus ministers. One highlight of the program, participants say, is when they lead weekend encounter groups of their own. Hundreds of people are on campus each of six weekends during the summer to participate in encounter groups for the benefit of our "trainees."

Sometimes on reaction sheets that we collect from weekend participants we read that they liked their group very much but thought the leader wasn't very expert, which, when we tell that to the trainees before their first weekend leadership experience, takes some of the pressure off them: that there can be a good encounter group even if they are not at the peak of their form. They can get the idea from this that an encounter group is what the people do, not an event that is attributable to the leader's cleverness. Nevertheless, it is understandable that these novice leaders will want to do well and will feel a nervous responsibility at first. Under this circumstance they are closely attuned to early signs of their success or failure. I recall an encounter group that I led shortly after completing my internship in clinical psychology and while at WBSI to gain postdoctoral encounter experience. Dick Farson, co-facilitator with Carl Rogers of the group filmed in "Journey into Self" (Chapter 4) and director of WBSI, was leading a group in the room next to mine. It was one of the first times I was on my own. My group was pretty good, I thought. On a coffee break the first day I bumped into Dick in the hall and told him with pride: "Three people cried in my group this morning!"

"That's nothing," Dick said offhandedly. "I had a woman vomit in mine."

I am cured of keeping score.

Another story illustrates the insecurity an inexperienced group leader initially feels. One of our trainees the second summer, going through the program with her college faculty member husband, was a woman of twenty-six who looked at least ten years younger. She told us in a meeting of the training community before the first practicum weekend that she was apprehensive about how the group would get underway: "I'm afraid people will come in on Friday night and look around and say, 'Who's the facilitator?' And when I raise my hand they'll looked shocked: 'How can a sixteen-year-old girl be the facilitator?' What can I do? What can I say to get the group going? I'm afraid they'll walk out."

"Why don't you tell them that?" one of the other trainees said.

"What?"

"What you just told us."

So she did. She allowed herself to be *met*. The group was an encounter from the beginning.

We think that an encounter group will go better with a leader who worries about what the group will think of him or her and who has the courage or foolhardiness or humanity to admit it to the people concerned, than with a leader who acts like an expert. An expert can easily intimidate participants into wanting to please him. We think an encounter group will go better—does, in fact—when the leader is willing to yield to the process, when the leader rises to the level of participant. With our inexperienced trainees as leaders, we think the summer groups are among the best that we do at our Center, an organization heavy with professional training on its full-time staff.

## The Psychiatric Philosophy

Now, as you can imagine, a program such as ours—with its person-centered model of leadership, with the concentrated participation of laymen—can worry those professionals who think that sickness is more important and more imminent than health. Of lay-led groups generally one mental hospital physician raised this question: "Can the nonmedical leader of a T-group [yet another name for encounter] be sure that he will not destroy a schoolchild's balance or bring insanity on him?" I love that question, because the answer has to be No. But you have to add, then, "Neither can the medical leader be sure he won't drive a child insane."

It is such a revealing question. What kind of life do you think a person has who worries about people producing insanity in one another? Would he want to lock up both sides to protect them, or just one? Would he be afraid to talk to schoolchildren? Or would he be afraid only if other people talked to schoolchildren? To render life by the looming possibility of insanity! Well, maybe that's what happens if you hang around mental hospitals. . . .

Sometimes it seems the doctors do all they can to reinforce our fears of the extreme possibilities: suicide, psychosis, and malpractice suits. One of the consequences is that people have learned to be cautious of one another when the going gets deep; they have learned not to trust their instincts. Now, if one considers that to be crazy is to be psychologically isolated, the doctors in fact *encourage* craziness by warning the rest of us to be careful with individuals who might go over the edge (and, as they point out, it's hard to tell who might go over the edge—it could be anyone). The greater the apparent need of one human being for others, the more "competent professional opinion" doubts that a layman should get involved. "Stand back. Let the doctor have room."

## The Leap

Many people, having gone stale in adult life—maybe Jerry of Chapter 4 would be an example—sense the need in themselves for some kind of breakthrough. This is one reason for the popularity of encounter groups and for the fact that frequently they are dotted with emotional incidents, such as Jerry's own tears.

The meaning of a breakthrough is that at its beginning a person doesn't know where he is going if he steps across the line, just that he wishes for once it would be possible to let go, no longer to control.

But what if he would do that and everybody would go away? How would he get himself back?

So a lot of people opt not to let go.

A breakthrough into health is very similar at its beginning to the plunge into psychosis. One leaps into the unknown . . . and doesn't know if he will land. When the events has a felicitous conclusion, one leaps and starts to fall . . . and someone is there to catch him. When the leap is into psychosis, one leaps and starts to fall . . . and he falls and he falls and he falls . . . and no one ever is there.

Precisely to the extent that people are so dreadfully fearful of having any responsibility in a psychosis and therefore back off from their teetering fellows, precisely to that extent do they make psychosis more likely.

"If ever I let go and start to fall," someone said, "I hope people will be there to catch me and to hold me." This cannot be solely the responsibility of doctors. There are not enough of them. They are not that strong.

## The Primacy Of Relationship

When I was in the practice of individual psychotherapy I once had a patient who would not cooperate. He would not be his problem. All he would do is say nice, safe, unrevealing, unfelt things to me and I would say respectful things back to him. It was very soporific.

I began to feel quite anxious. I had long had the suspicion that I was not a very exciting person. That I was passive. Evidence was beginning to gather with this man that it was so. I could help people who could maintain a level of excitement about being helped, but apparently I lacked the nerve to stir things up when we were trapped in a relational vacuum.

Weekly it was getting more deadly dull. I began to think of other means of making a living. Finally, I let the cat out of the bag.

"I'm feeling very bad," I told him one session, "very much like a failure."

He perked up: "How long have you been feeling this way?"

"It's not a new thing. It goes way back."

"Could you say more about it?"

Yes! You get the idea. We had changed chairs. He was the doctor and I was the patient—but it didn't matter! For suddenly the room was filled with excitement. There was a relationship!

He began to be cured, of course, and so did I. (It was only awkward when I tried to think of how to bill him.)

I have come to realize that it does not matter who is doctoring or who is patienting, that it is the relationship itself which is primary and healing. It can be approached from either end interchangeably.

When the issues are personal, as they are in therapy, as they are in encounter groups, helping is identical with being helped.

The particular potency of the encounter group, I realized, is that once it gets rolling, most relationships are approached from both ends simultaneously, and that there are many vectors of relationship going at once.

Typically, a group stays together long enough so that the members realize that no one is exempt from needing the others; and that everyone present, no matter how damaged, has unique personal resources on which the others can draw. There is thus a massive exchange of need in the encounter group.

Encounter groups are more potent for immediate personal change in participants than is individual psychotherapy, because, typically, in individual psychotherapy someone is hiding, exempting himself from explicit participation in the relationship, for the purpose of antisepsis, he says. Therefore, in individual therapy, relationship is often truncated.

Who is this hider? The doctor. It is harder for him to get away with it in the encounter group.

If the doctor is called out of hiding by the encounter and drawn into participation, who will be the guide? Each person as he is able, including the doctor when his own flavor of humanity suits the need. When the issues are personal, professional training, which ordinarily divides people into the able and unable, is the least qualifying element of leadership. It is one's humanity that counts.

A participant reports on such a group:

As to the role of the facilitator in the group, I can only generalize from the one group I have been in, but it seems to me a group can provide successful experiences if the facilitator doesn't try to manipulate but just allows the group to be and generate its own problems and concerns. After the initial shock of finding that our facilitator was not going to lead us or direct our efforts but instead was going to be an open, honest member of the group, the group proceeded and didn't seem to feel the need for someone to guide or direct it. I believe the group was stronger because of this and the encounters between members more meaningful and real. It also seemed to set a tone that all felt for what was real and what was contrived. The few attempts by anyone to interrupt the natural flow of group interaction were quickly recognized as phony and were ignored.

Such a view of leadership frees the facilitator to be as potent as he is. As a person. In the early going of a group, because of the title he brings with him, being himself the occasion for the group to meet, he may be a model for the others. He provides a poor model, indeed, if he keeps his person under wraps. By coming out himself, he makes it easier for the others to do this also.

I would not mean to say that there is no place, also, for whatever special skill the leader's professional training has given him. It is part of his person, too, as he comes to the group, and he would hide a part of himself to hide his training and to hide the fact that he comes there as the leader.

There are helpful things the leader can do to facilitate the development of the group, short of revealing himself. (It cannot be rushed, anyway; his moment of joining cannot be contrived, cannot be brought in as itself a technical move honed elsewhere, for the group will not allow itself to be fooled.) He can, as does Carl Rogers, pursue the difficult task of listening for the meaning in what people say.[1] Meaning is not easy to discern in the early hours of the group, as you will recall from the material presented in Chapter 4. Or he can look for the connections between the statements of different people, and he can point to those links in his responses, for sometimes they too are hidden in the early going. But eventually, when the group has achieved a sense of community, these special efforts can be dropped. The group might even request it.

## It Is Hard To Let Go

The more elegant the leader's routines, the more they cost him (all those years of training!), the more important he counts them to the wholeness of those at whom they aim, then the harder it will be for him to drop them once beyond the point of necessity, when a sense of community has arrived.

Few such routines are necessary in the first place, I think, but if they are harmless and keep the leader occupied and make him feel that

1. See his *Carl Rogers on Encounter Groups* (New York: Harper & Row, 1970), p. 47.

through them he can justify his presence in the group, then it is not bad to listen and to link. Only if it keeps him out of community is it bad. And then, I am going to say later, that is only too bad for him.

I directed this chapter primarily at psychiatry, because the medical men seem to have the most precious routines and the greatest stake in neither letting go of them nor letting anyone else in on them.[2] And, so the evidence seems to be, when you look at who controls, who complains about other people wanting to talk to one another and then wants to accuse these people of "practicing" "treatment" (and who therefore must hold treatment very dear and place it high above love and the other less trainable forms of interaction), you have to say that it is especially the psychiatrists who need to be reached and invited back into the human race. Encounter groups would be good for them.

It is hard to get through to them, however, because they are a strong and influential guild; why should they change? They have fear going for them and whatever need remains with us for a priesthood. Other professional groups even want to ape their style. Thus the clinical psychologists organize to protect their prerogative also. And the social workers, pastoral counselors, organizational development consultants, mental health technicians—I am therefore using the title "psychiatrist" for all those people, regardless of profession, who want to scare us about relationship and stake it out as their own commercial franchise, who push interper-

2. I don't mean to denigrate here the medicinal aspect of psychiatry, the part about the pills. I know nothing about that part—except I know my favorite quote about pills is this, from a letter written by a college student:

"I am in the hospital where I have been for the past eight days after surgery. Ugh! The number of pills they've got me on is unbelievable!! The minute I wake up in the morning I get a dose of Librium, which is repeated umpteen times throughout the day, not to mention an assorted variety of other pills including three kinds of headache pills, brown ones, yellow ones, white tablets, pink capsules, red capsules, green capsules, two-tone green capsules, pills to make me hungry, shots to prevent nausea, pills to make me sleep, shots to kill the pain.

"This morning my surgeon came in and I had the sheets pulled up over my head. He said, 'Are you hiding?' I said, 'Yes, from the whole world.' He said, 'Oh, you're feeling kind of bad today, huh?' I said, 'Hand me a gun and I'll shoot myself in the head, man!' He said, 'Well, we'll give you something to make you a little more active and cheerful, okay?' Add a few more pills. . . ."

sonal orthodoxies, and who mask their fears of revealing themselves in professional excuses.

To protect us from the incompetent practice of encounter, these specialists are moving to limit by law who can have a group. They want the groups under the control of the medical profession and the licensed others whose guild styles approximate the doctors', as though the doctors somehow know better how to live than do the rest of us. (Do I overdo the "live" part? I stress it so, because I believe the encounter group is a compact experiment in living. And I really do not know what body of evidence has been produced that indicates that doctors are better at life than others are. How could they be so good if they're gone from home so much?)

The problem the professional associations worry about and want to mount laws about—the problem of the competent facilitator vs. the charlatan, will take care of itself—unless we start issuing paper credentials of competence to professional friends and limiting group leadership to them.

The best aim would be to have the *world* certify facilitators, no paper, just word-of-mouth reputation. People would come to a good facilitator if they wanted to be in an encounter group. They would seek him out as part of their own personal moral quest, as in ancient times men sought out other men who were known to be wise.[3] Because the bad facilitator's groups would be no good, no one would come to him—until we confused things by building the facilitator profession, issuing institutional validations, implying that advanced degrees and training certificates are more efficient indices of trustworthiness than one's community reputation and what he is able to hammer out in meeting with his fellows.

Anyone who has been through a professional degree program knows how little it has to do with bringing out the quality of his person. It has more to do with supressing it. I would rather trust my neighbors to run encounter groups, particularly if many of them were doing it and thus

3. Were there "certified wise men"? My image is that the Sophists had certificates but not the wise men.

I had a wide choice among them, than limit leadership to people titled "psychiatrist" or "psychologist" or "social worker." My neighbors even include a doctor, by the way, and he is a nice man. I would let him run an encounter group. I'd let them all do it—and then I'd be very careful to whom I went and to whom I'd send my loved ones.

What if (impossible dream) everyone were set up as a group facilitator? What if everybody had a certificate? if at birth every person got a piece of paper from the state that said "licensed psychiatrist"—or, I'll give up my title, "licensed psychologist." Then we'd talk to those people worth talking to and we'd ignore the paper. We'd know it didn't mean anything, for everybody would have it.

## An Encounter Group Is A Shared Investigation

An encounter group is best seen as a joint human research:
"What way are you?"
"And what way are *you?*"
These questions cannot be answered easily.

"If you want an answer, you will have to stick with me. I cannot quickly reply, unless a superficial response will do. I will need your help in coming to an answer. You will have to help me—with me. If you will ask your own questions about yourself, that will help, too. Do let that inquiry also be open between us."

This process of shared investigation can go on whether or not everyone participates. It is all right if the doctor holds out. Others can go ahead without him. But if the encounter goes better the more who are there participate, then why does the doctor hang back?

Perhaps for the sake of clean living. Though he must withhold himself from human community to do so, as long as he controls his own decisions, the process and outcome of his life will be neat and predictable —or will they?

Consider Ivan Ilych, Leo Tolstoy's fictional nineteenth-century professional bureaucrat, who was concerned to cultivate the careful life-style. But in the end he could not elude danger. Once he fell heavily in a household accident, and later the injury became cancerous. The ultimate impropriety crept up on him. Ilych began to die. He suffered great pain.

It was true, as the doctor said, that Ivan Ilych's physical sufferings were terrible, but worse than the physical sufferings were his mental sufferings which were his chief torture.

His mental sufferings were due to the fact that that night, as he looked at Gerasim's [his footman's] sleepy, good-natured face . . . , the question suddenly occurred to him: "What if my whole life has been wrong?"

It occurred to him that what had appeared perfectly impossible before, namely that he had not spent his life as he should have done, might after all be true . . . his professional duties and the whole arrangement of his life and of his family, and all his social and official interests, might all have been false. He tried to defend all those things to himself and suddenly felt the weakness of what he was defending. There was nothing to defend. . . .

He lay on his back and began to pass his life in review in quite a new way. In the morning when he saw first his footman, then his wife, then his daughter, and then the doctor, their every word and movement confirmed to him the awful truth that had been revealed to him during the night. In them he saw himself —all that for which he had lived—and saw clearly that it was not real at all, but a terrible and huge deception which had hidden both life and death. . . .

For three whole days, during which time did not exist for him, he struggled in that black sack into which he was being thrust by an invisible, resistless force. . . .

Suddenly some force struck him in the chest and side, making it still harder to breathe, and he fell through the hole and there at the bottom was a light. . . .

"Yes, it was all not the right thing," he said to himself, "but that's no matter. It can be done. But what *is* the right thing?" he asked himself and suddenly grew quiet.

This occurred at the end of the third day, two hours before his death. Just then his schoolboy son had crept softly in and gone up to the bedside. The dying man was still screaming desperately and waving his arms. His hand fell on the boy's head, and the boy caught it, pressed it to his lips, and began to cry.

At that very moment Ivan Ilych fell through and caught sight of the light, and it was revealed to him that though his life had not been what it should have been, this could still be rectified. He asked himself, "What *is* the right thing?"

and grew still, listening. Then he felt that someone was kissing his hand. He opened his eyes, looked at his son, and felt sorry for him. . . .[4]

4. "The Death of Ivan Ilych," in *Great Short Works of Leo Tolstoy* (New York: Harper & Row Perennial Classics, 1967), pp. 299–301.

## CHAPTER 9:

# ARE ENCOUNTER GROUPS DANGEROUS?

There are psychiatrists who say encounter groups are dangerous. There are conservatives who say encounter groups are dangerous. I have said that the dangers are manageable, that people are so made that they can take care of themselves, but at times I am sure I have also seemed to be saying that encounter groups are dangerous.

I do not want to lay down a general principle, though I think the experience is common enough, but I have suffered a kind of personal jeopardy in encounter groups. I may be beyond it now, though I cannot be sure, for I seldom go to encounter groups any more. Still, I want to discuss the danger I see in somewhat abstract terms rather than too personally. You can take from it what squares with your own experience or with what you have seen in other reports, including those to be presented later in this book.

## On Being Dazzled By Possibility

If one has led a repressed life, his early exposure to an event so powerful as an encounter group can be confusing. Because now he sees

74

possibilities as attainable that before he had abandoned as beyond his reach. He can love anybody. He can be loved himself.

There is an important distinction to be made between possibility and potentiality. As a person and as a psychologist, I am concerned to come to use more of my potential and to help others use more of theirs. But this task can be thwarted by permitting my mind to range over my possibilities. I can confuse the two: *what is possible* and *the fulfillment of potential.* Possibilities are abstract. They are, for example, what I imagine that other people do. They are what I might envy. Potential, as I want to use the word, is within me.

A writer interviewed leaders of psychological growth centers and told me that at one place they wanted "to reinvent the wheel," that they had thought it was possible, in effect, to have wives in common. It turned out, on experience, not to be within their potential. One man interviewed, who favored the effort before it began, found himself to be very jealous, reporting that he even felt murderous at times. Potentiality has built-in limits by the nature of the matter with which it works. But, being abstract, possibility realizes no limits.

The new opening-up urged within the group movement needs balance. It is probable that more people could dare much more personal experimentation than they have allowed themselves in the past, that there is much more room for personal risk in the lives of most of us than we would have guessed. But one should not be fooled by possibility, for more things are possible than are within one's potential. A person could waste a lifetime dwelling on images of possibility and could lead himself astray.

I am thinking, if this example does not excessively offend by its lack of elegance, of the number of men who attack their babysitters. The number is not large, I am sure, but now and then one reads of a man being charged with sexual assault: He got too interested in the babysitter. Often, I would venture, such interest is not just sexual but expresses a longing for relationship, a longing that has no ground and thus no potential for realization: an empty possibility, one that will become actual only at the cost of attack.

If one considers possibility only, it is possible that the babysitter and the man could love one another. More improbable events than that are reported to occur. Someone does win the Sweepstakes. If the man allows himself to think about this, to dwell on the image of the possible, then he can confuse himself by losing rootedness in his own particular matter, a matter which in its final and liberal analysis cannot be named, but which is there nonetheless. Is it convention? Is it propriety? These are traditional names for it, but if a person thinks too much about the names, he is liable to tip the argument toward embracing the possibility, for such names are easily rejectable as old-fashioned. But "love" is never out of fashion. Within the framwork of the possible, there is no reason these two people couldn't love one another. They are, after all, two persons.

## Images of the Possible

Images of the possible can be compelling. Something must be said about the control of such images. Not conscious, effortful control, for if this is necessary the battle is probably already lost. Not control through deference to convention of through an awareness of propriety, for by now these virtues have become for us disembodied. I want to find something that these old virtues probably meant—although through endless, formulistic repetition they miss for us now—something about paying attention to what, who, and where concretely one is, and about not toying with every possibility that comes along, for the solid development of one's potential can disappear entirely in the excited pursuit of possibilities.

In its release of possibilities, the encounter group, in spite of its overriding goods, can get one to forgetting the reasons for things, or to rejecting the reasons for things, because of their old and inadequate names. In encounter groups, one can become attracted to possibility, at what he might later find is the sacrifice of some of his potential.

People in encounter groups want to see one another again. "Oh, if only we might live together," one woman said. Group reunions are planned and hopes expressed for individual meetings.

But these commitments usually turn out to be unattainable when put to the test. The promised group reunions seldom come off; the commitments made between individuals at the conclusion of a workshop rarely turn out to be grounded in more than a wish. And that may be right, for to spend much time with the wish would be unfortunate if it caused one to lose awareness of the ground at one's feet. The people given in a person's life are there, on the ground which he left to come to the group and to which he will return. That is where his potential lies. That is where his humanity is now to be proved.

It is good to try oneself out. Most of what I have said in these pages has been more or less about that. But one can be terribly distracted by possibility. "I can be more than I have been." What a valuable discovery, and how much better than always to feel determined by the past! But following the discovery, the subsequent task of finding where one's potential leads is one in which attentiveness to the ground will be a helpful companion; for on the blush of first rediscovery of potential one can be misled by possibility. "I'll tell you what's happened to me," a woman is reported to have said on a postencounter questionnaire: "I've left my husband and children. I'm working as a go-go girl and I live with an artist." Maybe that will work out, and maybe it won't; but that on her awakening it became possible, is not reason to have tried. A person will have to pay attention to his ground to find where he can go.

I think the group leader can help with this problem if he himself is willing to be vulnerable. It won't do to warn people. That has never been an effective means of moral education. But it may work through *contact*, through the group's knowing the leader's concerns through knowing his person. If the leader's concerns have community validity, this will emerge through contact.

## How To Lead An Encounter Group

Built into the leadership approach I have advocated is a protection against participants overwhelming themselves with the attraction of new possibility. This protection is that the facilitator himself becomes involved; in so doing, he will be much more aware of the life import of group activity through suffering that import himself. He will be unlikely to urge or even to stimulate group invention when he knows that he too will bear the process and consequence of the group's activity. He will be likely to let people *pace themselves.*

The facilitator may have said, before he had been in many groups (as did I), "I long to be more involved with people." And then, when the longing is realized, find that it presents more input to him and his given commitments than he can handle. So he learns not to wish too quickly for things because in an encounter group they can happen. He becomes less willing to quickly assert what he wants, finding it better now to wait attentively, to discover what it is he wants in a gentle interaction with others, remembering, also, that his life goes on beyond the group.

Though less an involvement in one, potentially sticky sense, this is an involvement nonetheless, an involvement that is not so likely to carry one away. It is a multidirectional involvement, in which everyone learns at once, everyone together, and in which respect for the discovery of new limits is built in, through respect for what the nonexpert among group members can offer, who are perhaps closer to life for being less imbued with the encounter culture.

The group is in a better position for multidirectional, life-implicated learning if the facilitator is in it with them than if he is exempted, standing back, arranging for them to go into areas that he hasn't charted himself or will not bear the consequence of exploring.

My point is not that one kind of experience should be arranged rather than another, a cautious one rather than an experimental one, but that nothing need be arranged whatsoever. What is needed is an occasion for meeting. It will happen if the leader will allow himself to be met. In so doing, he does all that is necessary, all that is justifiable, to make the occasion for others also to meet.

And that is enough, for when people meet, they are made to grow.

# PART IV

# The Effects of Encounter
# Groups on the Individual

## CHAPTER 10:

# THE IMPACT OF THE ENCOUNTER

Are encounter groups effective? Yes, sometimes almost too much so. Let me tell you of some evidence.

Two of my colleagues at the Center for Studies of the Person have teamed up to measure the effectiveness of Jerry's group for immediate change in its members. One, Carl Rogers, invented a process scale that is capable of measuring changes produced in individuals during psychotherapy.[1] Used by raters working from tape-recorded segments of therapy interviews, the process scale judges the changes in individuals along a number of continua, ranging from rigidity and closedness on the lower end of the scale to flexibility and openness at the higher. The scale is built on the hypothesis that healthier individuals are willing to risk more openness and flexibility than those who have less psychological health. Another colleague, Dr. Betty Meador, adapted the process scale for use with encounter groups, measuring change in each of the members of Jerry's group over its sixteen-hour weekend workshop.[2] Her raters

1. C. R. Rogers, "A Tentative Scale for the Measurement of Process in Psychotherapy," *Research in Psychotherapy* (Washington, D.C.: American Psychological Association, 1959).

2. B. D. Meador, Analysis of Process Movement in a Basic Encounter Group (Unpublished doctoral dissertation. U.S. International University, 1968).

worked from brief segments randomly selected from the film of the entire workshop, and each group member was given a "process rating" for each half of the five group sessions.

Are encounter groups effective? In terms of immediate process changes, unequivocally yes. Typical of results with the process scale used on recordings of individual psychotherapy is van der Veen's finding that the average amount of process movement from first session to last is 0.9 on the seven-point scale for clients whose therapy was judged successful on other criteria.[3] This is for a course of therapy sessions averaging approximately a year in length. For Jerry's group (his group was not unusual; the finding would be similar, I would predict, for other encounter groups), averaged across the eight members of the group, process change from the first hour to the last was two full points out of seven. This in a weekend!

Jerry himself moved four full points on the seven-point scale, from an initial rating of 2.6, one of the lowest in the group (quite rigid, quite distant from feelings) to 6.6. Such a large amount of movement, *more than four times the process movement one typically makes in a year of successful individual psychotherapy*, is not unequivocally a value, coming as it did all at once. We did not have follow-up data on Jerry, but from the documented experiences of other individuals, we can reconstruct the kinds of experiences he might have had after the group.

## Pain . . . And Hope

One man, not unlike Jerry, said later, "I was told I was hard like a rock, though I didn't feel the things I had been through. They warned me that if I were to be open I would begin to feel. And it is true. The succeeding events have been painful and traumatic and I have felt lonely." But then he adds, hopefully, "The association of my friends has

3. F. van der Veen, "A Strand Scale Analysis of the Psychotherapy Process Scale," *Psychiatric Institute Bulletin* I (Wisc. Psychiatric Institute, 1961), pp. 1–11.

also become more real. Those I thought I was helping are the ones who have been sustaining me and I love them more for it."

Having found a new, expressive self in the encounter group, and a new responsiveness from people there, Jerry might be very disappointed when getting back to his own setting. He might expect more of people at home than they can give immediately. In the encounter group, a person learns that he can speak of his personal realities and, initially to his surprise, finds that people do not turn away after all—and that eventually they show that they need the same concern he does. But without the special safety of the encounter there are risks indeed in expecting concern or even of offering to give it: the risk of appearing foolish, of speaking of a personal reality and finding it is not true for anyone else after all (at least not that you can tell), the risk of saying what it is difficult to say and finding out that people do, after all, turn their backs. A participant wrote of her reentry at home after a particularly intense encounter experience:

I reach out to hug the people I love, and they quickly hug back and move away. I want to hold them, but they're embarrassed and uncomfortable. I want to look in their eyes while we talk and their eyes dart away and glance and dart away again.

The hardest thing is to try to share my encounter experience. I hear the words I'm saying and realize with dismay that they don't mean what I mean. I come across like an evangelist or a free-love advocate when what I'm trying to say is loving and caring and closeness. I find myself getting quieter and quieter and I keep my hands at my sides. I'm even getting polite. After only three days I say, "Yes, thank you, I had a lovely vacation." Then I feel an ache in my heart and I want to cry out, "Where are you, Paul and Al and Marilyn and Maura?" I want you back and the sound of the guitar and the arms around me and the faces I love.

People at home don't know for sure what has happened to you when you have been in an encounter group, if they haven't been in one themselves; and they hesitate to believe that what appears to be the case actually is so, that you are in fact inviting them in. They can't respond. Thus, the letdown for the participant going home can be acute.

And the effect can also be traumatic for the individual who is left at home. Another woman wrote after what was for her a successful encounter group experience, "I still haven't come down to earth and the good feeling continues. I'm almost afraid of what will happen if it evaporates." And then she tells of her situation at home:

> For the past year or two I had been experienceing an estrangement between my husband and me—a very subtle feeling, nothing I could put my finger on. Things like, he would tune me out when I talked about things at work, so I stopped sharing my day's experience with him. And we really had not been talking with each other enough.
>
> When I went home Wednesday evening in my euphoric state, I wanted to share this with him—I felt pushed away physically. I think I was afraid to have a basic encounter that night, that it might burst my bubble. So I went to bed. The next night was it—I came on like gangbusters. *I* made love to him. (I've always shied away from doing this. I'd always felt that the man should be the aggressive partner. I now realize I had been cheating both of us.) Naturally he responded to this and we were up until 2 A.M. talking. I had never felt so close to my husband before—and we've been married seventeen years!

Her husband can be pleased with her new ardor. But he can also wonder, "What went on at the workshop? What happened that you should get so turned on?" Another woman, whose postworkshop experience was quite similar, wrote, "My husband said, 'What did those people do to you anyway?' I said, 'They just loved me. That's all. They loved me.' His hurt was visible and instantaneous. He said, 'Wasn't my love enough?' "

The person who remains at home can feel very left out; he can feel that the participant's loyalty is now to individuals who are strangers to him, to the group members rather than to himself.

Indeed, the participant can miss them greatly, those new group friends of whose love he is absolutely assured (because he held back nothing but was loved anyway). "I find myself looking at people coming toward me now and trying to make them a familiar face or figure," a participant wrote. "Then there's a shock of disappointment when it isn't one of us. I can't believe you're really gone."

## The Upsetting Quality Of The Encounter

Upset can occur within an existing relationship where one participates in the encounter and the other stays home. But there is also a kind of upset for the individual participant himself, a need to integrate the powerful encounter learnings. At one-thirty in the morning the night his group ended a graduate student wrote:

After I got home, all I wanted to do was lie down and rest. I felt at a really low ebb physically, even though the group itself was not a strained, intense one. . . . I went to bed early, as much from a desire not to fool around with books and studying as anything. I wasn't tired. In fact, I am still so turned on it is fantastic. I feel like my head inside is just bursting with activity; my body tone hasn't relaxed yet, ideas occur with great rapidity and many of them get extensive treatment. Plans are made—I have been planning things that I ordinarily would be afraid to commit myself to, making decisions, etc.

The upset, I think, can be characterized like this: it's as though we spend most of our lives learning, to our regret, that people are not like us after all—and we even begin to doubt that *we* are like ourselves. At times of deep feeling, we know that the things we want in life are simple —to be loved, for example. But as we look around, it doesn't look as though anyone else wants what we want, for no one seems to act that way, at least not when they appear to know what they are doing. Then gradually we give up on having what we want and instead settle for less, becoming now a little isolated, even from our wishes for ourselves.

But suddenly we learn in encounter that what we wanted was valid after all. Not only for ourselves but for others too. It is bound to be upsetting, to learn this so suddenly. It can cause one to lay awake at night as it did the graduate student.

It can be painful. A student who was in several encounter workshops at her college wrote: "Our group experiences woke me up; they have kept me awake for a long, long time and they won't let me go back to sleep. And I'm so tired." She now sees in people what she could not see before, and she wishes she didn't. Every new meeting is a test:

I have recently become increasingly aware of how great an effect those blasted encounter sessions had on my deepest self, because now I have an extremely trying experience every time I meet somebody new. I am painfully aware that under the appearance of each individual I meet is a person, and that this will probably never be shown to me. . . . I've seen the insides of people in these groups and it is so very difficult to accept the other part they show normally.

In the face of people's hiding, of which she is now aware, she is reluctant to risk showing the person in *her*, either, but she finds that her old ways have also been disconnected: "I took a professional modeling and charm course once—it taught how to be poised and a great conversationalist —and I can't do that to people any more!"

In light of this report, it is not surprising that "I damn those [encounter] sessions whenever I meet a new person."

But then she adds, "I don't say I'd trade my new feelings with people for what I had before the groups. Something is awake inside me now that was asleep before."

Her awakening caused her great pain, and not many participants report themselves being *that* upset by the encounter, though some degree of upset seems endemic to the experience. In spite of the pain, however, many participants say what this student said: They would not trade back for their preencounter attitude. "It was upsetting, yes," another student reported, "so much so that I don't want to be in another group for now. But I have no regrets, for I learned something very important. I learned what people are like, and I won't forget it."

My own early learning from encounter was similar to that of these students: I learned about other human beings. It was a learning more useful to me than painful. I did not participate very actively in my first group, but I was changed from it; as I sat there I sensed the damagedness in people of whom earlier I never would have guessed it. I saw that even the most formidable façades could "crack." I don't mean this in a violent sense, but that underneath even the slickest fronts were persons like me, who were not very sure of themselves after all, who at times felt very small. For me it was a powerful learning. It made people approachable. And when the right time came it made me willing to let others also see the damagedness in me (for it turned out I had been one of the worst offenders, never letting on that I was anything other than what I wanted to be). I am not afraid now to approach people, and not so afraid to be known.

## A Schema For Change

It will help to put into sequential perspective the typical effects of encounter on the individual.

### What Causes the Encounter Effects?

A young man wrote after an intensive encounter that his newly opened door, the door to his private room that formerly had been closed against the world, stood for the event of the encounter. We had done an encounter workshop in the seminary where he was a student, and he wrote to us two weeks later that neither the seminary nor he would ever be the same again. He was willing to share with us some notes he jotted down within four days of the workshop. In sending them, he wrote that they sounded somewhat maudlin to him from his perspective of two weeks, but added that he really wasn't writing them at the time for anyone other than himself:

I have been freed; I am a free man and I *feel* it—an integrated feeling. I not only *know* that I am free, I *experience* it.

This is a wonderful feeling. It pervades my whole self; it radiates outward and includes others: I respect and cherish their freedom; I wish all others to be free and to experience freedom.

I realize that I am free of guilt feelings, that I am happy for the first time in twenty-five years. The hurts that have accumulated since I was a child all have been exorcised. How? By the loving acceptance of the group. For one long moment I trembled beneath the terrible fear of being stared at and judged by my peers. But then I wept, hesitatingly at first, then fully—from the depths. My past pains came to the surface; I relived and sloughed off the deep anguish of loneliness. No thoughts, no desires entered my head. I was feeling throughout my entire person—body and soul. It was bliss. The others wept inside with me; I felt it—I felt them. I didn't understand or judge what they were saying, but each word and emotion that bore it slid into touch with my deepest self. As each of several in the group said in his own words, "I love you, Joe," or "I'm sorry, Joe, for the pain I've caused you," new tears came, deep sobs that cast up and out the wall of fears, the self-pity.

The unconditional acceptance of the group, this "I love you, Joe," does not mean "I have regard for you in every way; here you can be any way you want, and it will be okay with me" (for that would be not to care); but rather means "I love you just because. You don't have to do anything now to win my love." No performance standards. It is right that I love you, because you are lovable; and if you loved me, that would be right too.

The confidence that comes from knowing that one does not have to perform to be loved, rather that he just has to be—this confidence is not liable to go away quickly (of course the rush of emotion will go away that comes with the realization of love). In transmitting his notes from the encounter, Joe wrote to us that, "Now, over two weeks after the intensive encounters, there has been a notable lessening of felt happiness in me as an individual (and in the seminary a dissipation of the common glow of warmth). Within myself some of the old struggles and indecision have returned. And yet the basic peace and security remain. I know I am loved and that there is about me something basically lovable. No longer am I afraid to speak out in public; the disapproval others may have about what I say doesn't bother me or keep me from speaking out."

## The First Phase of Change Following Encounter

To know that you are loved, just because, is the powerful event of the basic encounter group. Typically it leads to a three-phase development. First, having perhaps several days to bathe in the afterglow of the workshop experience, the individual wants to cause some of that glow in his own life. For a while, somewhat self-consciously, he begins to live by a new norm, in contrast to what likely was his old norm of caution. The new norm is one of revealingness. He wants to dare in his life what he tried in the group and found valuable there.

At this early point following the group, it's a little like swapping an old game for a new one. He has to apply a bit of force to himself in order to be different than he was before the encounter, for slipping back into old ways occurs quickly. He issues internal reminders to try himself out in the new "encounter way," and his friends can probably read it in him, the less happily for not having shared the encounter experience with him: "Looks like he wants the whole world to be an encounter group."

Some college students of my acquaintance complained that their friends who had attended an encounter training program came back to the campus of a mind, evidently, to shock people. " 'Shit' seems to be their favorite word," one of the students said. "They're going around here bashing people with openness: 'Let me tell you how I see you,' uninvited—that sort of thing."

Open or just loving, the encounter participant's behavior may look phony to an observer at home at this early point. At the least it will be lumpy: The seams will show as the encountered one tries out his group learnings in the less permissive world of day-to-day living and as, sorting and discarding, he makes up his mind about what is useful in the encounter experience beyond the group setting.

Although an annoyance to his friends, the task of the first phase is an urgent one from the participant's viewpoint. From inside, his experience is one of having been awakened. He sees that the world is hedged around with artificiality, hiding the love, and that he had accommodated to it in the past. He can accommodate no longer. Having settled for a cautious way of life before the workshop, he will not settle any more, for he has learned the settling not necessary; he has learned in the workshop that what he deeply wants is what others want too; he has learned about the value of taking risks: that the spontaneous reaction of people who are free will be to like him more for taking risks, not less. But having learned this, for a while following the group experience risk-taking may become a kind of compulsion. Not wanting to back off from what he learned at the workshop was possible, the participant now *makes* himself take risks.

## The Crisis Phase

And it leads to a crisis. People threaten to walk out on him, or he on them. The crisis eventuates because in dissatisfaction over the disparity between what-he-learned-in-the-group-was-possible and how-the-world-continues-to-be, the individual finally sets out to change the world or make his own. The world resists both tactics and a crisis occurs.[4]

The typical crisis is short-lived, however. Yes, a competition has developed between the old community of the encounter participant (e.g., his home) and that new community he carried with him from the workshop, his encounter group. But though the encounter group is a powerful community, it will win out only temporarily over the participant's other commitments, because (unless he becomes what can be

---

4. The *Wall Street Journal* (July 14, 1969) reported two such crises under the headline, "Some Companies See More Harm Than Good in Sensitivity Training":

. . . a division manager in one big company was described by a source familiar with his case as "a ferocious guy—brilliant but a thorough-going autocrat—who everyone agreed was just what the division needed because it was in a tough, competitive business." Deciding to smooth off his rough edges, the company sent him to sensitivity training, where he found out exactly what people thought of him. "So he stopped being a beast," says the source, "and his effectiveness fell apart. The reason he'd been so good was that he didn't realize what a beast he was . . ."

And in another case, a woman, division manager in a consumer products company, was sent by her company to sensitivity training, where she really liked the openness between people. But:

". . . I came back to work and found it shrouded in the usual unnecessary tactfulness and diplomacy. I discovered that the training had so opened me up that I was tired of the Mickey Mouse." When her superiors wanted to delay a decision on a new product development program she had been working on for more than a year, she told them that she was tired of their procrastination and quiet to take a comparable job elsewhere, where she has more latitude.

To protect its own interest, the woman's company eventually dropped sensitivity training for its employees, and the manager mentioned first was replaced, since, no longer a beast, he was no longer effective.

called an encounter bum, going now from group to group, living only on group weekends in the woods and no longer at home), the encounter group exists only in memory, and commitments to other groups, such as family and work, no matter how sterile, have more reality than the initially powerful but now diminishing memory of the encounter.

## The Third Phase

The life crisis ordinarily dissipates the first-phase compulsivity, the lumpy learning trial period; you get slugged in the crisis and you back off for a while, but you have learned. And what you are left with is not just a memory of a good time and then some rough times, but with a residue of new knowledge, new attitude, and new hope: of in-chargeness in your own life and of your potential kinship with other human beings. Like Jerry, for example, you know now that people can be concerned. And like me, you know that people feel damaged inside. Both knowledges can make you less afraid. Having experienced that you can touch people, you have a new personal power, a power that you will not abuse, however, for that you can touch people anywhere is identical with the fact that you can be touched.

This residual learning from the encounter is enough to last a lifetime. It's what encounter groups are all about.

This learning has two aspects to it, a substantive learning, not unlike that which people make in psychotherapy, and a procedural aspect.

*The substantive learning.* People take from encounter groups a learning not unlike what they might pick up in a successful course of psychotherapy. It has to do with a new capacity to get close to what is going on inside oneself, a capacity to contact that source of authority in oneself represented by feeling. One participant said, "It's like knowing what's happening inside now and where I'm at. This helps in itself, even though I might not be able to change it. It helps just to be able to know what I'm feeling." He adds, "Part of it is to look inside of me, and part of it is in how I relate to other people."

It is in learning new ways of relating to people that the danger of "encounter phoniness" comes: learning new ways of talking to people (learning to say "shit"), new ways to impress them (with openness). But in learning to be more in touch with oneself—that is where there is little risk of perverting a genuine experience into a showing off. Here a person can take new experience and use it for himself, to grow as he wishes. Encounter groups are more part of the tradition of moral education than they are the scientific tradition of psychology or the medical tradition of psychiatry, for they have *most* to do with learning to be in touch with oneself, and with becoming more of what one wishes to be.

*The procedural learning.* Procedurally, one learns that he can call on people. One participant, having moved beyond a desire to be in more encounter groups, able now to have the same goods in his own life, looked back on the group as a protected environment: "You can have experiences in the group and realize relationships there that even with the same people outside are impossible. The encounter group is a bit of a cocoon."

*Yet what you learn is that you can make a cocoon when you need it.* Yes, one would be misled if he thought that all the world had the same kind of safety as the encounter group. The encounter group is a special occasion. One learns, however, that he can create special occasions when he needs them.

The group permits relationships to develop as close and as openly as they do precisely because it is not an everyday occurrence, and he who thinks that somehow his everyday world will be like the encounter group is in for disappointment, or is liable to phony-up good feeling later that really isn't there.

The good feeling of the encounter group itself and the burgeoned self-confidence that is an immediate effect of the encounter group—these do dissipate in time. But a person learns what he can do about it when he needs people: He can call them together.

Jerry said, "I learned that this could happen not just here but any place I want it to happen." The foremost learning of an encounter group is this procedural learning, that one can call on people. It is no small learning.

What has one achieved, ideally, in the third phase of encounter learning, the phase that follows the crisis? He has achieved an expanded range of choice. He can be more present to people when he wishes, and more private also when he wishes that. He can be in charge of his life through being more aware of where he is; that is to say, less compelled by his habits, with less need to defend against his experience, with greater sensitivity to the full range of feelings all people have. One of the interesting facts about the long-run effects of encounter groups is that, after going through the considerable kinds of trauma I have been describing, individuals often wind up looking much as they did before the encounter. But with a difference. I know it in my own life: this time I can *choose* to be the way I am, and I can sense in myself the real possibility to be other than how typically I am, if *I judge that to be appropriate*. I am no longer compelled to be some one way only. One could not ask for more.

So pleased was he with his encounter learning, one participant even printed it on his Christmas card:

I have become excitingly aware of my own uniqueness and my right to be myself, and I realize that only I can make those decisions which govern my life. I realize how much of my life and the lives of others is wasted through inaction or dishonest action in an attempt to seek approval. Open, honest communication between persons with a positive regard for oneself and others is my only hope for happiness, so long as I am true to myself and allow you to be true to yourselves. My wish for you who wish it too is that you can live your own lives. I hope you can feel free to do those things that make life meaningful and full. When you want to laugh, I hope someone else can hear it. When you feel like crying, I hope there is a shoulder offered for your comfort. If each of you can live your lives freely, you will help me to do so too.

# PART V

# The Effect of Encounter
# Groups on Systems

## CHAPTER 11

# THE NIGHT LUCY SAT ON THE CHICKEN

Sister Lucy was so rattled when her students said they loved her that she sat on her chicken dinner.

She had risen from her place on the couch in the school encounter lounge to compose herself in private following the revelation of their love, and she was still so flustered when she came back that she forgot where she had left her take-out chicken dinner. She sat on it, and it greased her religious habit.

I suppose you could say that her habit got so thoroughly greased that night that she started rolling and has not stopped since.

This is what happened.

We were invited to do encounter groups over a three-year period with faculty and administrators and students of a large Catholic school system in California, schools staffed by the religious sisters of the Order of the Immaculate Heart of Mary. When we started the project, which we called one in educational innovation, there were 600 nuns and 59 schools: a college, eight high schools, and fifty elementary schools. Now, four years later as I write, a year following the formal completion of the project, there are two schools left and no nuns.

We did some job.

It wasn't all our doing, of course; concurrent moves away from authority and structure within the Catholic church influenced the most dramatic results of the project; the long existent, very progressive ways of this unique order of sisters were influential; and it is difficult to separate our findings from the fact of growing disaffection with institutions in the larger culture. But I want to tell about our project, for the direction of its effects, I believe, are indicative of what will follow elsewhere when the free encounter group is made a fact of organizational life.

Carl Rogers initiated the project with his article, "A Plan for Self-Directed Change in an Educational System," in which he proposed that encounter groups, which had proved successful in changing individuals, also be applied to our stagnant educational institutions.[1] "With the world changing at an exponential rate," Rogers said, the goal in the education of young people today "must be to develop individuals who are open to change, who are flexible and adaptive, who have learned how to learn, and are thus able to learn continuously. . . . The goal of education must be to develop a society in which people can live more comfortably with change than with rigidity." Rogers continued:

> But such a goal implies, in turn, that educators themselves must be open and flexible, effectively involved in the process of change. They must be able both to conserve and convey the essential knowledge and values of the past, and to welcome eagerly the innovations which are necessary to prepare for the unknown future.
>
> A way must be found to develop, within the educational system as a whole, and in each component, a climate conducive to personal growth, a climate in which innovation is not frightening, in which the creative capacities of administrators, teachers and students are nourished and expressed rather than stifled. A way must be found to develop a climate in which the focus is not upon teaching, but on the facilitation of self-directed learning.

Fortunately, Rogers asserted, the means to facilitate such learning is at hand in the encounter group, which has proved effective in fostering self-direction within individuals. But a social system must be provided that will sustain those individual changes and not, as at present, seek to

1. *Educational Leadership*, May 1967, pp. 717–31.

undermine them. Experience has shown that the encountered individual returning to a conventional organization has had only two alternatives: "He returns disappointedly to his previous conventional behavior, or he becomes a puzzling and disruptive influence in his institution, neither understood nor approved," for his new commitment to being fluidly personal is far out of tune with what the organization traditionally has accommodated. Therefore, it makes sense to attempt the massive application of encounter groups to an entire system. Hopefully a new process-centered organizational style will emerge that will accord with the new ways of valuing to which encounter participants become committed.

The first element of Rogers's plan was to be an encounter workshop for administrators and board members of a school system:

> The group . . . will be relatively unstructured, and if past experience is any guide, exploration of current interpersonal feelings and relationships will become a major focus. Often gripes and feuds which have for years prevented real communication come to the surface and are resolved in the eight or ten hours per day of intensive group meetings. The encounter group provides the administrator with a microcosm for studying the problems he faces, and the problems he creates, in his own organization. Through confrontation he discovers how he appears to others. He also has the opportunity for experimenting with and trying out new modes of behavior, in a relatively safe situation.

The next steps would be encounter workshops for teachers, for class units, for parents, and, finally, combined groups of teachers, parents, board members, administrators, and students, both active and drop-out.

Rogers urged that the groups be held within a reasonably short period of time "so that the impact will not be dissipated," though admittedly there was thus also the possibility of too rapid a change and, ultimately, of rejection by the community: "It cannot be denied that when problems, especially interpersonal problems, are faced openly rather than being swept under the rug; when interpersonal relationships are substituted in place of roles and rules . . . then a certain amount of constructive turbulence is inevitable."

The possibility of turbulence was one challenge of the project to those who worked on it and those several school systems that quickly expressed an interest in being part: that together they would yield to a highly personal process of communication, rather than a controlled experiment in which leaders knew what would happen. In this experiment, outcomes would not be fully predictable. The plan would substitute "the problems of a process-centered organization for those of an organization aimed toward static stability."

This was to be the most exciting kind of research, a little like gambling, a "what if" kind of research: "What if you got people to talk with one another in a school, really to notice each other? What if colleagues sat down with one another without a topic to discuss—and if they promised to keep at it beyond the typical ease and then the typical boredom of falling back on small talk? Would it be dangerous for them to be personal with one another—or would it be freeing?"

"ANY TAKERS?" Rogers asked in capital letters in closing his article. Although he had been trying to get funding through government research agencies for two years, within a month of the article there were numerous takers, including two individual donors, Charles Kettering II and Everett Baggerly; a small southern foundation that supplied the largest portion of the funds, the Mary Reynolds Babcock Foundation; the Merrill Trust; and, most importantly, the school system represented by the nuns of the Immaculate Heart order, ideal partners for us because of the comprehensive nature of their school system and the commitment of their leaders to the goals of Rogers's open-ended research design.

We set to work. First, in the summer, before the opening of school and the first workshops scheduled specifically for faculty, we held a series of encounter sessions for members of the order. Two hundred and fifty nuns volunteered to participate. They included the delegates to the order's forthcoming policy-making convention, the body that would pass the liberalized rules that would later prove to·bring the nuns into open conflict with the cardinal-archbishop of Los Angeles. There were six workshops for the nuns that summer, and the initial reports indicated again the potency of the encounter method. Over the years of their membership in religious life, frustrations had built up among the nuns that had had no communal opportunity for airing. Now, with the groups, Rogers's prediction that participants would find opportunity to work out among themselves feelings formerly buried in "gripes and feuds" was proving accurate. "I'm scared," an official of the order wrote, "for I know that this is only the beginning, and I really had no idea of the amount of hurt or repression or lack of self-confidence or backlog of isolation which had been there for the releasing. But where only disappointment existed prior to the workshops, now I see a lot of hope and positive effort underway. What can we do next?" Of the six workshops held for nuns, only three had initially been scheduled. The others were added because of demand created by the immediate impact of the first ones. This burgeoning of interest followed by multiplication of effort was to be typical of the early months of the project.

With the opening of school, there were encounter workshops within the faculty of each of the Immaculate Heart schools that was willing to participate. Lay faculty members were included in these groups along with religious. The plan was to have one workshop for each school, on a weekend at the order's resort conference center; six to ten weeks later would be a follow-up weekend. Participants would have time to try out encounter learnings in work settings and, in the second round, to bring up new problems that might have arisen.

Beyond these initial two-part faculty workshops, no more groups were on the schedule. Since the project was to be one in self-direction, if there was to be more encounter activity it would be at the request of first-round participants. It would depend on the experience proving valuable to them.

It did. Faculty members and students volunteered by the dozens following the first round. Groups were held in classes, among departmental colleagues, in the administrative council, the student newspaper staff, the student council. In one month following the opening of school, there were twenty separate encounter groups at the college alone, all by request.

Sister Lucy's was one of these. She taught a course in educational methods and invited a project staff facilitator to come to an early session of the class, hoping the students would develop a sense of unity in the encounter. Here is the facilitator's report:

The workshop was scheduled for four hours. We planned to send out for dinner and to continue to meet while we ate.

We got off with a bang: one of the students, who is now doing her student teaching, complained that all her college career she has been required to take courses, ostensibly to learn techniques which will be necessary in her teaching, only to find that the actual course is quite different than the catalog description. "How can you insist that it is necessary to learn methods of teaching when once we get into class we find we aren't learning any methods?" She went on this way for a while, repeatedly expressing her resentment while the group listened and tried to help iron it out. The problem really didn't seem capable of resolution; and then she came out with her real resentment: "Look, it's not courses that are on my mind. What's really bothering me is that I found out my parents don't want me to marry the boy I want. He is Jewish. They have raised me to have good judgment and have said they are proud of my judgment, and now they don't accept my judgment concerning my own happiness." She wept as she said it, and from that point the group moved along quite on its own energy.

At one point in the session, about an hour from our appointed time of conclusion, Lucy, the instructor, said, "I don't really feel a part of this group —some of you still insist on calling me Sister." She said it with considerable feeling in her voice, but as she continued to talk about it, seemed to back away from the feeling and seemed once more, as is her way, to want to be helpful rather than to be helped. Finally she got around to talking about how impossible it is for her to say that she needs anyone, particularly her students. "I can't say those words," she said.

It was obvious that she needed all of us, but that she couldn't do anything about it herself. So at that point I put down my dinner, crossed the room and sat beside her, taking her hand and putting my arm around her. She started to weep. Choked up, she said she couldn't speak and that she was absolutely frightened now of what they would think of her. At that point, one of the male students, who was sitting on the other side of her, also put his arm around her. I went back to my chicken dinner because I knew then that what was necessary was being done: Lucy, who could not say she needed them, was being held in the arms of one of her own students.

You will know from Chapter 4 that this is what an encounter group can be like. Our hypothesis, in the words of an early report, was that when people in a school—administrators, students, faculty, it doesn't matter—sit down "to get to know one another as persons, in addition to their role functioning in the school, then this kind of 'personal knowing' will lead to a freeing of creative capacities: defensive communication will be minimized, people will find likeness in one another and will thus find it less necessary to protect themselves, their feelings, and their hunches—all potential sources of creative action."

There was immediate and stunning effect. A month after a workshop, one student wrote to us of her experience:

The workshop was one of the most important and beautiful experiences of my relatively short lifetime. I am very much changed in my attitude toward teachers, fellow students, and just plain everybody. I'm far more open (or at least I try very hard to be) than I've ever been.

In some subtle but absolutely shattering way, even little crummy ordinary experiences seem intensified now. I'm sure this is due to the fact that my focus is on people instead of things, and I'm equally sure that it was the encounter that switched the focus for me.

I get so *excited* about everything now. The greatest thing in the world to me is talking to someone I hardly know and realizing—with a shock every time—that we share a world in common. . . .

But it's hard, even now, to express verbally just how wonderful the experience has been. The whole thing gets caught up in the beauty of the people and the place and the time, and I usually end up crying. . . . All I can really say is that you gave me the chance to learn how to look, to listen, and to love. I give you back a big hunk of that love when I say thank you.

But then a curious thing began to happen. People began to back off from one another. They began to disown their experience. A student who wrote glowingly of the beauty of the encounter and its immediate aftermath a year later authored a critical editorial in the student newspaper:

. . . WBSI is, in plain language, using the Immaculate Heart College Complex as a guinea pig.

This conjures up visions of mad scientists performing hair-raising experiments on unsuspecting victims. Unfortunately, the actual explanation of WBSI's reason for being here conjures up even wilder visions—simply mention the phrase "sensitivity session," for instance, and watch the reactions of people who consider themselves relatively secure in their sense of well-being.

What had happened? I want to try to explain it in following chapters, as best my colleagues and I have been able to figure out, for then we may learn not only of the effect of encounter groups on institutional life —an effect which if we had to name it with a single word would be "disruptive"—but also learn of the prospect for the spontaneously personal being welcomed within the normative American institution, a prospect that, I must say, I now see as rather dismal.

## CHAPTER 12

# THE EXPERIMENT

## The School System

Of the fifty-nine schools staffed by the Order of Immaculate Heart Sisters as the project began, two were owned and administered by the order itself: the high school and college, which shared grounds with the order's Mother House on a corner bordering a residential section of Hollywood. The other schools were located in seven different Catholic dioceses on the West Coast and were owned by the dioceses themselves, the largest number controlled by the conservative cardinal-archbishop of Los Angeles, James McIntyre. The cardinal and the sisters had been on uneasy terms with one another for years.

Comprising the teaching staffs of the combined elementary schools were 375 sisters and 183 lay people. Staffing the high schools were 115 sisters and 94 lay people.

The full-time faculty of the college, where most of the work of the project was to center and the data to be gathered, numbered sixty, evenly divided between lay and religious, with men making up not quite half the total. Lay faculty held approximately a third of the departmental

107

chairmanships and the positions of dean of faculty, business manager, and director of admissions. The college was eager to point out its open character, in face of the typical pattern of control in Catholic education: "Sisters who are appointed to College faculty posts have prepared for and earned their positions. Once on the faculty, they compete on equal footing with lay faculty for tenure and advancement." By and large this self-report accorded with the college's reputation, which was one of openness, competitiveness, and creativity. The college was best known for its irrepressible band of art students, led by the serigrapher Sister Mary Corita.

There were 500 undergraduates at the college, 300 full- and part-time graduate students, mostly in education. As the project began, the college was for women only. As it ended, coeducation was gradually being introduced.

## The Project Staff

From the project's beginning to its conclusion, there were more than sixty staff members, the majority serving as facilitators for the numerous encounter groups. A dozen, headed by Carl Rogers, were full-time staffers of the Western Behavioral Sciences Institute, home base of the project when it began. The others came from the ranks of the human relations professionals and others who volunteered. There was an industrial psychologist, for example, the psychologist-rector of a large Jesuit academic community, several clinical psychologists in private practice, a cadre of advanced graduate students, and several housewives. Our criteria for staff selection included group leadership experience with WBSI personnel. But beyond that, selection was on the basis of personal qualities: Was the facilitator sufficiently secure to yield to the same encounter process in which he wished group members to become involved? Was he relatively nondefensive? Was he beyond the need to push people around or have them display themselves? We wanted a gentle kind of group, a soft leadership, the kind of group any of us on the staff might have been willing to risk for loved ones of our own. We didn't want the group leaders to make anything happen; we didn't want them to tell people what to do or how to be; we wanted the encounter to be only an unstructured relational occasion, allowing the participants themselves to decide what would follow.

But many on the staff came at this work from backgrounds in the practice of intensive psychotherapy or, more generally, intensive weekend encounter work with stranger groups. We had developed habits of going for emotional depth. We wanted to do our best work on this project. We wanted to have a powerful effect on the system—Rogers had announced that he wanted the workshops close together so that our experimental effect "would not be dissipated"—and initially that meant that we offered what we were good at, the intensive personal encounter as we had developed it with stranger groups.

## Procedure

We began. There were the planned initial faculty workshops for elementary and secondary schools. The college faculty turned over its annual preschool orientation meeting to us, and we encountered for two days, the fifty-five participants divided into four groups. In a private report, Rogers summarized the tenor of these college faculty groups:

[Since] the main thrust of the encounter group toward greater openness and expression of feeling tends to run contrary to the assumptions held by many college faculty members, . . . in each of the four groups, as might have been expected, there were varying degrees of willingness to participate in "an encounter" in spite of the fact that all members attended voluntarily. The staff tentatively analyzed the interaction in the four groups in this way: in two of the groups those participants who were reluctant themselves to express feelings also made it difficult for other members of the group to do so. They sometimes warned against expression of feelings. In another group, there were those who wanted the exploration of feelings for themselves and others who did not wish this kind of experience but the choice was a personal one and each side was willing to respect the choice of the others. In the fourth group, by chance, the members seemed by and large to be of one mind about trying out the kind of openness and exploration of feelings implicit in the encounter group idea. . . .

In spite of this mixed success of the opening faculty workshop—mixed, that is, on the encounter model that had become habitual for us, in which participants willingly risk their feelings with one another—the requests for workshops for classroom groups, for students, for departmental meetings and the like began to pour in. We met every request and had a steady flow of facilitators commuting to the Immaculate Heart schools.

What were the groups like? Very like encounter groups as described earlier in this book. There were Jerrys and Rozs. There were such events as Sister Lucy crying in the arms of one of her students. There was gentle growth and there was hostile, long-postponed confrontation. And sometimes there was reluctance and resistance and so little encounter process that the meeting seemed an utter waste of people's time. The report of a staff facilitator highlights the different flavor of two elementary school workshop groups:

> There seemed to me quite a different atmosphere pervading the two groups. My first group was quite well prepared for the type of encounter that took place. A couple of the sisters from this faculty had been to the summer encounters for nuns and thus had had some experience in a group. The workshop was offered to the faculty in a very permissive way, with no stigma attached to those who decided not to participate; and from what I could gather, there was absolutely no pressure put on people to attend. While I have been associated with groups that have moved faster and explored deeper levels, I do believe this was one of the better groups that I have worked with. . . .
>
> The second group I worked with was quite different. Two of the members came expecting a workshop in new educational methodologies, with some lectures and demonstrations on improved ways of teaching children. A couple of the group participants had been to a prior group, which for them had been a fairly negative affair, or had had contact with people who considered their own group experience to have been wrenching, and had raised considerable anxiety in the others about what might take place. A couple of the members had had positive experiences in previous groups. There was also a lay faculty member who

was extremely anxious any time the conversation got on a real feeling level, and actively disrupted this type of conversation whenever she could. She was very difficult for many members to cope with and very threatening to some. It was not until the last session that she actively engaged herself and took a more permissive attitude, to let others more fully explore some of their own feelings without interference from her.

Few of the groups were as free and as low-key as this facilitator's first one. We were suffering a bit, I believe, not only from our own enthusiasm for the notion that encounter groups could reform education but also from the enthusiasm of those who had earlier had good encounter experiences. Our original summer workshops for nuns had grown from three to six on the reaction of those in the first ones who said, "I have friends who simply must do this too." And while some of the participants in the fall workshops had been warned to expect a hard time, I now believe it was our eager *supporters* who made the work more problematic, who with their persuasiveness altered the voluntary character of the workshops. "In many schools," a facilitator said, "I got the word that there was a real stigma involved if you did not sign up, and that people were unaware they really had a choice about whether they could attend."

Encounter groups were suddenly what one *had* to do. It was not the best atmosphere for gentle growth.

CHAPTER 13

# FOR AND AGAINST

Let us look within the sequence of two weekend encounter workshops for one of the Immaculate Heart schools.

At the sisters' conference center in the resort of Montecito, near Santa Barbara, a December encounter weekend was held for an elementary school faculty. Two months later there was a follow-up weekend. A senior member of our research team, a highly regarded facilitator, led the group together with a younger staff member.

## The First Round

This is the senior staffer's report on the first-round workshop:

. . . It was one of the most moving and emotional two-day sessions I have ever had. . . . The group went quite quickly into personal things, some of which were very emotional indeed. Here is the most outstanding example:

During the late afternoon on Saturday, when I thought the session was drawing itself to a comfortable close, people began to confront one of the sisters with the fact that she seemed to be a little too sure of herself, and that perhaps this was evidence of insecurity. Suddenly, an older lay teacher, who had been a constructive participant in the group, picked this up and began to really attack her, saying she was "much too good, too good to be true. You're just like my sister."

Sister Bernice was really hurt and began to weep. Then the older teacher suddenly blurted out a very traumatic experience of her childhood, and it became clear that in attacking Bernice she was really attacking her own natural sister, whom she felt had repeatedly betrayed her. Tearfully she revealed an early experience. . . .

This set off a period of sobbing which must have lasted twenty minutes. Bernice, who had been attacked, came over and knelt beside her, and they wept together for a long, long time, with the group able to do nothing except sit by in silence. Finally it began to subside and the two women were on better terms. The older woman, however, would not look at the group, feeling that she had told them something much too shameful. I told her that if she would only look up she would see nothing but concern and sympathy on the faces around her, but she could not look up. She left the room. The principal, who is a very sensitive woman, immediately took after her, but we had no idea if the older teacher would return, because she seemed so deeply upset.

As soon as the two of them left, one of the lay teachers turned to me and said indignantly, "Do you think this sort of thing helps anyone?" She was joined by several others who admitted that they had been so shaken by the experience that they wanted to get up and run but simply did not dare. . . . I and several others tried to explain that if a person had held such a secret all her lifetime and felt so badly about it, it might really be helpful to her to share it with others —but that admittedly it was hard for the group to take.

Several people said they were just shivering with fear. I suggested we move into a smaller circle and hold hands quietly for a bit, which we did. I thought the group would close on this note, when we heard footsteps approaching, and here were the principal and the older teacher back to join the group. The teacher obviously felt so much better that she even wisecracked a bit and joined the circle holding hands, starting to explain some of her reactions. But I said, "Don't say anything. Let's just sit and hold hands together." We sat there for some time quietly, with a real feeling of closeness and with a great deal of satisfaction in the fact that we were all a group together again. . . .

## Immediate Effects

When later interviewed, participants reported immediate effect in their lives. One of them, who in the group was very obviously bothered by the emotionality, reported, "Afterward, it was really horrible. I couldn't get home fast enough that Sunday. I ran into the house literally screaming and crying. It took a long time to settle down. . . . The workshop just didn't seem real. God, it was emotional. People were saying things they didn't really mean."

Others also reported themselves to have been disrupted—but in positive ways. One said, "When I got back from the weekend, I simply could not teach. There were too many things going on in me. So I told my children about my experience and tried to convey something of the spirit of the thing. They were fascinated and some of them even wept as I told them about it. Since then the class relationships have been ever so much better. They see me as a person and I see them as persons. They come to me much more often. They come to me for hugs and love. It is just fabulous what has happened in our class."

## The Second Round

Of the twelve participants in the first workshop, only eight chose to return two months later for the follow-up. The dropouts were all lay teachers, one whose husband prohibited her returning. But three faculty who had not participated the first time now decided to attend. One said, "I came because I saw so many changes in the group that I wanted to find out for myself. They were so much closer to each other after the workshop. They seemed to communicate on an entirely different level. I also heard a lot about the workshop itself—good things, people who were upset, people who had negative feelings—and I wanted to see for myself."

The second-round group was not as emotional as at the first. But there was a fair share of the usual tears, and the focus of the group gradually shifted from one member to another. By Sunday, most of the new members of the group were being given specific attention in turn. The senior facilitator's report captures the flavor of the final day:

Millie, another new member, was next in the group's focus. She is living with her mother. She feels her mother could not possibly get along without her, yet her mother turns all her own anger and irritation and pent-up frustration on Millie. So she dreads to walk in the door when she gets home from school. She seemed to have the feeling that she must devote her life to her mother, even though it destroys her as a person.

The group helped Millie realize that this was *her* problem, that her mother could get along perfectly well (as confirmed by Millie's own report that she had done so on several occasions), and they pointed out that perhaps it is Millie herself who would have difficulty being independent. Millie agreed. She said she often wished she could just be a happy child.

She is very fearful of becoming independent, though recently she has taken some steps in that direction, her attendance at the group being one of these.

In the final meeting, Sunday night, Joann was the first major focus. One of the priests in the group confronted her with some of her lack of feeling. The group all chimed in on this. It was fantastic to watch the slippery and elusive way she could avoid ever expressing herself or any of her feelings, always focusing either on intellectual things or on some other member of the group. As the confrontation became more and more direct, she said she just didn't know what was being asked of her. Finally, however, she admitted to being griped at many of the things which the principal does and particularly at her emotionality. She expressed her positive feeling for the priest, though she felt she had to remain aloof, "because of my position." She resented some things that Millie said to her. She interacted in a real and emotional way with my co-facilitator, and finally she wept a bit, became more feelingful, not so quickly defensive in her reactions. Several members of the group, but particularly the principal, practically cheered when she expressed some of her feelings. They had felt that she was so cool and aloof.

One of the members had brought a bottle of bourbon. It was broken out at this time and there were very affectionate—and some critical—reactions to each other, very spontaneously shared, meaningful, and warm. I then asked Nan, the sister who had not attended the previous weekend because she had been ill, whether she wanted a chance to say anything, because she had been very quiet, though very attentive and sensitive throughout the sessions. Very hesitantly, Nan put herself into the group, as a shy and sincere person. She got a great deal of affectionate and positive feedback. She really became a member of the group.

It was very difficult for the group to break up. There were many embraces and the feeling was very, very warm.

## Further Effects

Three weeks after this workshop, the co-facilitator visited the school to observe and to interview the personnel, both those who had participated in the two encounters and those who had fled after the first. For himself, the interviewer had seen the workshops as positive events:

I felt that both sessions accomplished a great deal in terms of positive individual experience. The early encounter had deep and moving moments. As a result, participants reported changes in their own behavior, better personal relationships, and experimentation in the classroom and elsewhere.

Although the second encounter started slowly and was less dramatic and emotional than the first, it moved well and by the end seemed personally rewarding to all the participants. It was a very useful follow-up to our first meeting, and I marveled at some of the changes I saw in people.

Nan said that though the experience wasn't without its disruptive aspects, the gains outweighed the disruption. "The good feeling at the end made up for anything negative that might have happened earlier. I was expecting something hideous, and it wasn't that way at all."

Not having attended the first weekend, it was hard to get into the group for awhile and for a while it seemed contrived. But on Sunday I felt much more at home; I didn't feel left out. I came out really elated. The support was fantastic.

A few days later, however, reality came back; the feeling of support had evaporated. I got depressed a week afterward; the good things that happened seemed then a passing event.

But now [three weeks later], I no longer feel depressed. The principal and I have become much closer. I am comfortable in a group now. I don't feel like I have to say or do something. Whatever I do, I know it's okay and that I am liked and cared for.

The interviewer was heartened at this reported growth in Nan and at evidence of similar changes in other individuals who attended the workshop. But then, when he attended the weekly faculty meeting, he was surprised to find "little indication that, *as an organization*, they had been through a sensitizing experience." The discussion at the meeting, he reported, "was abstract, lacked direct confrontation, was marked by a skirting of issues, and was rife with innuendoes and indirect references." There was a very apparent split on the faculty; most of them liked the workshops and what happened to them personally, but others were still frightened and angry. "I feel closer to some of the people on the faculty," one teacher said, "but I can't judge that we feel more a part of a common effort." Another, one of the four who attended the first workshop but refused to come to the second, said, "If everybody feels they got so much out of it, why can't they function better as a group?"

## Evidence Of Organizational Conflict

Even in the early months of the project, we began to accumulate evidence that this sort of split was fairly general. It seems a highly personal value issue was involved in the very idea of the workshops. Some of the participants were pleased and excited by their own participation and enthusiastic about repeated and wider encounter opportunities. Others, a minority but a vocal one, felt compromised by the groups and were bitter that the school system had casually agreed to three years of such deep, personal experimentation.

Whatever their private enthusiasm for the groups, the project supporters who were in administrative positions began to become uneasy, because they were increasingly aware of a new source of dissension within their faculties. To keep the peace, a few schools dropped plans for second-round participation.

The attitude of one of the high school principals was typical. She said that she valued her own personal involvement in the encounter and knew that many other individuals profited also. But, our interviewer reported, "she has reservations about the effect of the groups on this school as an institution. Heading the school, she is concerned about faculty members being destructive or hurting one another. She is concerned about those who had negative group experiences and who then may disrupt the system. Her reservations are mostly administrative, but they are nonetheless real." The principal decided to have no more encounter workshops. "She wants to try to keep a lid on things for now, since relationships on the faculty are strained."

## The Supporters

However, after the first round at the college, the groups had spread quickly before opposition had found its voice. With the students joining in the groups, the camp of encounter enthusiasts swelled. Trying to control the sudden strong student interest in encounter groups was like trying to control dating, the college president said, "only in this case the students have fallen in love with themselves." Students were understandably enthusiastic, for many were making exciting personal gains in the groups, gains in individual functioning akin to those made in successful psychotherapy, without having to admit any need for therapy. In describing her own gains, which will be recognized as typical of encounter participation, a student said:

Before the group, I wanted to be good to myself, but I didn't know how to do it. Now it seems I know. I don't have to defend myself so much. Before, I would come up against somebody and I'd get the idea their opinion of me wasn't my own opinion of myself. And it would worry me. Now I don't have to worry about it, for secretly I know there's me. I know who that is. And, honestly, it pleases me.

Such gains, made also by faculty participants, showed up immediately in the form of shifts in emphasis within classrooms. Of one college class, whose instructor had been in several encounters, a student reported,

> I'm in a literature course which I can honestly say is a suffering class. Every single novel we read is not explicated in the old way—symbols, style, the author's intention—but we delve into the character as a person with *feeling* and we try to find an element of identification between that person and ourselves. There is a human pushing, pushing all the time. Sometimes I come out of there and I feel like I really want to cry.
>
> I'm saying it's a good class! But my heart is small. Sometimes I come out and it seems like my feelings are just clinging to my heart, trying to get inside. Sometimes I want to throw them away for the time being, because I've got lots of other things.

Sometimes it seemed they *had* to throw the feelings away in exhaustion. If the new commitment by project supporters to the feeling dimension of learning annoyed those who remained unmoved by encounter, neither was it easy for the supporters themselves to bear. It involved them in a style of honesty and intimacy that was wearing and from which any one of them might momentarily back off, to the confusion of the others. Sometimes an encounter advocate would find himself alone, unpredictably isolated even from those he thought were his colleagues in the feeling quest. One desperate supporter wrote to us:

> It was shattering to me to see that every single person in the group returned to his same role after the encounter weekend. Our daily relations are exactly as they were before the encounter group, the masks are all on again. I have invited them to my house, have tried to reach out to them individually, strongly implying nonverbally, "Don't you remember what we shared?" No response. I feel cheated. I feel like a child who trusted and believed and then is told, "Didn't you know it was all just a game?"

To account for the disparity between the personal closeness of the weekend and the isolation that occasionally followed, a staff member hypothesized a "Monday Morning Phenomenon":

> One might come to work on a Monday morning following the excitement of the weekend encounter, look around him to see if the others would acknowledge

the workshop's reality, and find them not doing so. Then, thinking it was not real for them and not wishing himself to be exposed as foolishly taken in, he would himself don the mask labeled Untouched. To the extent that each person was playing this Monday morning game, he might look around him and inwardly whisper, "It meant nothing to anyone but me." And, observing him, the others could say the same.

The hypothesis is supported in the experience of the older faculty member who had "sobbed for twenty minutes" and frightened people in the elementary school group described earlier. She wrote to her facilitator, "The first week back at school was a nightmare for me. As I saw each person, I had a horrible sense of guilt. I kept thinking how I had triggered the sensitive spot for almost everyone, and I had a feeling of being just a meddlesome old biddy." One can imagine that she would want to back off quickly, that she would hope the others might pretend the weekend didn't happen.

Alternatively, when such a system of pretense did not take over, when someone made his excitement about the weekend plain rather than hiding it in hope another might show first, then Monday morning could see an immediate recovery of the weekend's enthusiasm, the faculty flying too high to get to the work of the school. On another school encounter project, for a seminary that held a workshop for faculty and students, we found that it was weeks before a semblance of normality was restored. An interview team visited the campus and reported, "The students said they couldn't study for two weeks after the workshop because they were watching one another. Someone would say, 'Bob's in trouble. Let's go help him.' They would drop their books and go help Bob with his personal problems. It went on around the clock."

## The Opposition

At Immaculate Heart College, tension had begun to run very high concerning the project. A student leader said, "Living in the dorm, I hear people who can't even stand the word 'encounter.' They're really harsh. They just scream, 'Damn it, I want nothing to do with that!' But there are others who feel the exact opposite. You know, they live for it." Faculty were becoming sharply divided. The popularity of the new experiential classes was itself a cause of tension. "You find a lot more students wanting to sign up for the experiential classes now than for the more traditional lecture classes," a student said. "Attendance is down quite a bit in the lecture courses. I think it must be hard for those teachers."

Yes, it was hard. Faculty were feeling pressure from students to abandoned hard-won, long-developed lecture styles and to turn themselves into classroom facilitators. A report from a student who had been in three encounter groups describes a volatile situation:

Finally I am free in two classes to do something I like! Both these courses are constant reminders to me of our encounter sessions. . . .

I am afraid I am going to grow more and more dissatisfied with other classes because of Dr. Brown's seminar—last week we talked extensively about the problem of boring classes and apathetic students and the whole structure of the educational system—and because of Dr. Allen's free-wheeling approach to learning (no exams, books to read only if we are interested, papers on which we place our spontaneous, unedited, unparagraphed, unacademic, unimpressive reactions —if we want). With freedom in these two classes and, in contrast, so much regimentation in my class with Dr. Nutin, whom you've not encountered, and a theology class with reading as dead as the old scrolls, I'm getting very itchy —all sparked by you fellows.

## The Group Way—The Institutional Way

If faculty were increasingly upset by the pressure inherent in the popularity of the new teaching styles, many were also deeply troubled by what they heard went on within the encounter groups.

The reputation of our own school of group facilitation is as the most gentle of the various approaches to encounter. In spite of this, our groups were experienced by some participants as far too probing. One said, "As I sat in my group, I felt, 'My God, it will soon be my turn. He's going to focus on me next. He's going to start digging at me.' " When an individual fears that his weakness may be discovered, he will be wary of being called out, of being looked at or spoken to with directness. But more than such defensive fragility influenced people's reservations; there was also our own habit of going for depth. The more we were emotionally direct ourselves, hoping the groups would go better through our own participation in the risk, the more the resulting depth gave our critics points to make in arguing the unwholesomeness of the institutional encounter.

In organizational life, when interpersonal problems arise, the norm is to push them away; a light remark initially is warranted in the face of interpersonal trauma within institutions. But in the encounter group the norm is to go into that which is interpersonally awkward. And thus there is immediately a conflict between the group way and the institutional way. In the institution one fends off trauma; in the group one enters it. A faculty member who supported the original idea of the experiment commented: "A few people seem to have been through very traumatic experiences in the groups, and those experiences are what is now dwelt on around here. There is a lot of trauma in ordinary living, too. But maybe the people who are opposed to encounter feel that the groups are *setting up* a situation for trauma, and that this is a bad thing to do."

There are feelings that are better left unexpressed. There are issues that are better left unexplored. This is what the critics could say, and they could cite evidence. "For the first time in my life," a teacher said after her group, "I tried to be really honest with my mother. I told her exactly how I felt about the things which had been building up between us. Now my mother thinks I am against her. My honesty just made things worse."

One can empathize with that complaint, for surely there are manifold instances in life where speaking honestly has hurt one or another party to the expression. Yet anyone who has sampled the elation that can come with saying something honest-but-previously-reserved—and not getting rejected after all—such a one can literally ache to do it again; to be honest is to hold out the possibility of involvement, but letting people alone so often leads to the pervasive alienation sensed in institu-

tional life. A conversation between a project staffer and a departmental
chairman at the college illustrates the tension, and the way in which this
faculty member typically resolved it. The faculty member said:

A lot of us have to be assured that you don't want to make us over; that if
we want to keep on operating the way we do, it's okay.

*I for one couldn't assure you of that. When I get into relationshp with some-*
*body, it does matter to me how they are. I really cannot honestly say, "It is okay*
*with me that you are whatever way you choose to be." If he was really choosing*
*to be that way, I suppose it would be fine. But. . . .*

Yes, I know. I have two feelings on that. And one of them is from the
viewpoint of the school: I look at people from the same department, for example,
and we are different in our personalities, in our specialties; we emphasize different things as far as character development. Some people, for example, will say
to students, "You must always come on time." Others will put emphasis elsewhere. And I think this diversity among faculty is a good thing for students.
They can pick up something from one faculty member, something different
from another. Whatever a student picks up goes into the formation of the whole
individual.

*And the more he's got to choose from, the more he can decide for himself, huh?*

Yes. But when *I'm* with those people and I'm trying to communicate something to them, I find it very difficult to rub up against an atitude or a way of
acting that makes me respond in their way. When I'm with a power person,
particularly someone who seems defensively that way, it's very frustrating. Then,
typically, I either just join in the game and go along, or I withdraw from that
person. But what I *wish*, is that he would be different. So I see what you mean
about wanting people to change. But that, for me, is at a personal level, not at
the institutional level.

The contrast between the encounter style of communication—*enter-*
*ing* trauma, speaking personally, *not* leaving people alone—and the
typical institutional style of going around it all made our work very
questionable to those who had strong senses of institutional loyalty. Also
grating on them were the pressures that the enthusiasm for encounter
brought to bear on the faculty who hung back (for they had been told
that participation was voluntary—and suddenly they were participating,
like it or not, with all these encounter buffs in their classes and in the
faculty lounge and in departmental meetings, all forgetting decorum and

saying with deep sincerity, "Tell me how you *feel!*"). This combination led to an increasingly angry, highly placed opposition to encounter groups in the Immaculate Heart system.

By the end of the project's first year, many of the faculty who had long been influential in shaping institutional policy had chosen the negative in the issue of whether or not to encounter. And the negative side was now calling on its own outside expertise. A faculty member submitted a letter from a foundation official who had a poor opinion of encounter types:

> . . . please advise Father Hickey that . . . I am in complete agreement with him in the conflict you describe between the Rogerian faculty and the "squares" such as himself. (Fie on *you* for having an identity crisis over the issues and wanting to belong to both camps.) I attended a *Daedalus* meeting last week and got so bored with all the personality kids and their soul-searching that more than ever I retreat to the conviction that adding all of one's personality problems to the pursuit of knowledge and wisdom really furthers the enterprise very little.

This is not an inaccurate summary of the viewpoint that finally carried the day concerning our work. Encounter wore out its welcome quickly. Its advocates wound up lumped by the cleverest of the opposition with "the personality kids and their soul-searching."

## Encounter Slows Down

It came to be agreed in the Immaculate Heart system that the encounter project be deemphasized. The groups were simply too controversial. After the first six months' rush of activity, there was a significant slowdown in the spring, and then very little encounter work for the remaining two years. Changes had occurred in individuals and would persist, but these were personal changes and changes within the individual's own immediate areas of influence. The changes that occurred within institutional relationships themselves were largely disruptive.

I wish to paint an honest dim picture of the effects of encounter groups within an educational institution. But not everybody agrees. Carl Rogers sees positive institutional effects, as do yet several people at the college who worked closely with us.[1] But the effects they see are not the immediate result of encounter; rather they are due to the later organizational innovations of individuals who were personally pleased with the encounter and who wanted to provide for a freer institutional flow of personal data. None of their innovations, however, have direct lineage to our free-form encounter groups. If our experience can be generalized, we will have to say that when people try encounter groups in institutions, they will quickly want to stop, for encounter groups are disruptive of institutional life.

## Positive Outcomes

It is not inappropriate, however, to sample the positive side-effects of the encounter project. While the direct effects were organizationally negative, there were indirect positive effects.

For example, there is pervasive evidence in the project of changes in teacher classroom behavior following encounter. Wherever one can be king of his own hill—as the teacher in his classroom—he can make positive work changes following encounter; he is able to come on stronger with people when that seems appropriate and also more able to yield than before, in both cases because of the enhanced self-confidence that comes from encounter. A college student commented, "It used to be that Dr. Brown had to say jokes all the time, to keep things comfortable for himself in class. But he doesn't have to do that any more. He really listens to you now. He says, 'Maybe you're right' when you correct him or you add to what he says. It's no act, either, because what he says later shows that he remembers what you told him." Follow-

1. For a brief summary of his view, see *Carl Rogers on Encounter Groups* (New York: Harper & Row, 1970), pp. 142–44.

ing encounter a person's sense of success no longer rides on whether or not he has made a mistake. He can make one and admit it. Having become personally known in the encounter—"If my friends know who I am, why do I need to worry about doing everything right?"—he is free to be more fully a person, free to experiment personally within his sphere of responsibility.

One elementary teacher wrote to us about the more personal manner of teaching religion she tried after her encounter workshop experience. The day she wrote, she said, she had been talking with her thirty sixth-grade students about what they had heard her say to them in class the preceding day. "I commented on the fact that no one had heard me say that I liked them—that they meant something special to me. (The previous day I had actually named children in the class who really came across to me.)"

. . . Then I thought of Laura, a very bright little girl who never enters any discussion. I asked her why she didn't talk up in class. She didn't answer. I was most patient for a change and continued talking to her—and still she made no response. So I asked if anyone would answer for Laura. Mamie raised her hand! I told Mamie she had to answer for Laura as Laura would answer, and I would call her Laura. Gee, was it ever exciting! Mamie spoke so thoughtfully for Laura, and finally Laura interrupted her and explained where Mamie was wrong! Well, Laura talks all the time in class now. . . .

A teacher can become much less fearful about speaking to people with directness in a classroom after encounter. No longer does he pretend that individual, noticeable human beings are not present but only the group in general. The teacher can say, "I see you!" and the student can say, "Yeah! It's good, ain't it."

The primary organizational effect of encounter groups thus is downward: from the person who has been encountered to those with whom he already has some potency.

But the effect is not broadly horizontal. And decidedly it is not upward. It is a foolish subordinate who uses his new encounter freedom to challenge his boss—unless he is prepared to leave the organization.

## On Leaving

And, of course, leaving occurs, too, following encounter: One tries for a while to change repressive institutional policies and has whatever influence he can in his immediate work sphere, and if institutional life doesn't loosen he may say, "Who needs it!"

### The Nuns Leave

Just as individuals make long-postponed changes in their own areas of personal influence following encounter, so too might an entire organization in its area of influence. While the established norms of relating were upset *within* the Immaculate Heart schools by the encounter experience and intraorganizational strife surfaced, there was a new organizational confidence with respect to the outside world.

The nuns had been in conflict with the cardinal-archbishop of Los Angeles for years. Their progressive ways had long rankled him; and though he had striven mightily to keep them in line, for him they continued recalcitrant. From the nuns' own perspective, they had often compromised with the cardinal, giving in to his conservative manners, and still they could not please him.

They fought over the matter of dress: "Leave those blinders on!" came the voice from the chancery when the nuns announced a change from hard coif to soft. They fought on common schedule: "You will rise together, when I click the cricket, and go to bed when I click it again." They battled on common prayer: "How can you call yourselves 'religious women' when you give up daily Mass?"

But we are here concerned with the schools. The nuns had long made sacrifices for Catholic education. Large numbers of them had postponed their own professional development to fill the need for immediate staffing in the parochial schools. Many had been forced to begin teaching before completion of baccalaureate degrees. Without degrees and without teaching credentials, they were at the mercy of changing patterns in the church; if the schools were to close—and there was some chance many of them would—the nuns would be without jobs and without the formal qualifications to transfer into public education.

In their prevailing mood of enhanced self-regard, the Immaculate Heart nuns now decided to take care of their own. They told the cardinal that they wished to withdraw forty-three of their members from the Los Angeles diocesan schools to return them to college to complete their state teaching credential requirements. Not just self-interest was involved, the sisters claimed. "We desire to upgrade the quality of teaching service by the Immaculate Heart sisters. We reiterate the paramount importance of effective Christian education in fulfilling the teaching mission of the church." They went on to ask for more reasonable class sizes (fifty-child classes had made the Catholic schools infamous in educational circles), for full-time principals in their schools, for more money to upgrade lay teaching staffs, and for "the acquisition of adequate teaching materials."

The cardinal countered. He announced to the press that the sisters had issued an ultimatum. "They have given me a list of demands. They have told me they will withdraw from the diocesan schools if I do not agree to their demands in toto. I cannot in conscience agree. I therefore accept their resignation."

"Wait," said the nuns. "You misunderstand. Our requests are negotiable. We made no ultimatum."

"Oh, yes you did. Besides, I'm not talking to you," said the cardinal.

So the nuns cried Foul and prepared to depart the schools.

"The real point of difference between us and His Eminence," the sisters informed parents of children in their schools, "is not the proposed educational reform which is presently in the public eye but is our known intention to experiment with a new mode of religious life, as authorized by Pope Paul after Vatican II":

From our conferences and correspondence with the Chancery Office, we are convinced that one condition for our remaining in the schools is a return to our former way of life. The question of uniform dress is an obvious but minor part of the discussion. More central to the discussion are regulations for a fixed time of rising and retiring, fixed hours for prescribed prayers, a highly centralized mode of local house government and other points of like nature. This mode of living may have suited former times, but it is a hindrance to present demands of apostolic life. . . .

With God's help there will always be an Immaculate Heart community, and as long as this is true we will want and need your support and affection. We will continue to serve in our community-owned schools, Immaculate Heart High School and Immaculate Heart College. We promise you our own devotion and our continuing prayers. . . .

But just not all at the same hour.

And they prepared to leave the official structure of the Catholic church, to get out from under the organizational authority of old men from across the sea who never had seen them or their work. Immaculate Heart *Community* it would now be, no longer the Sisters of the Most Holy and Immaculate Heart of the Blessed Virgin Mary. It would be a community, in time, of both single persons and married, admitting men to membership as well as women.

And three years after they left, a year and a half following the retirement of Cardinal McIntyre, the new Immaculate Heart Community was welcomed back into the schools of the Catholic diocese of Los Angeles.

The community was smaller now: 280 as opposed to the nearly 600 members when our project began, but their heads were held very high indeed.

Why do I mention "our project" in this connection? Wasn't it the nuns' doing, the radical changes they had made? Wasn't their departure precipitated by events that began long before we came in contact with them? Yes, and in our early reports we specifically disclaimed any causal connection to what had happened. But knowing persons close to the community told us it was not quite so. A long-time faculty member of the college wrote to remind us that we had conducted an encounter workshop for the delegates to the sisters' convention, the body that had passed the reform documents that brought them into public conflict with the cardinal. If individual self-confidence emanates from an encounter experience, then organizational self-confidence might also:

It would be unrealistic to think that the two events, the encounter project and the conflict with the cardinal, just happened simultaneously. . . . I think we need a clear sifting of material to show, if possible, how Encounter Facilitated Revolution in a Static Society. Such a report should end with an offer to fly a team of facilitators to the Vatican. . . .

I don't think you can ever be blamed for what happened, nor can you take credit; but you *were* there. . . . The one conclusion that can easily be drawn be anyone is that you facilitated the action.

CHAPTER 14

# IN WHICH I ATTEMPT TO
# ACCOUNT FOR THE DISRUPTION

The consensus view of those involved—the people of the schools and of our own staff as well—is that the encounter project was very disruptive to the Immaculate Heart system. Having concentrated my own group work and later inquiries at the college, I am familiar with the case there. Because the college people were naturally more interested in the quality of the changes produced in their environment than in the exigencies of an honest research test, their own official focus is now on the fact that we failed them: we didn't know before we started that the encounter groups wouldn't work.

Here is their recent summary of the project:

. . . our stated trust in the individual and his right to control his own development and destiny didn't fit with the premises upon which collegiate structure and operation had traditionally developed. . . .

To meet unusual needs, we tried unusual procedures. In the fall of 1967 . . . we embarked with psychologist Carl Rogers on a . . . campus-wide experiment testing sensitivity training as a tool for creating a climate of self-directed change within a college.

Perhaps we should have expected the resulting implosion. The psychological stripping represented by sensitivity training proved to be balm for some. But for others it only heightened the distance between our current aims and the scholarly intellectual tradition. The treatment was too much, too soon, perhaps, and it became something of a fetish along which lines were drawn and the campus divided. Suspicions were bred and, most damaging of all, a growing intolerance of opposing views. Few quarreled with Carl Rogers' ideas. Many took issue with the disciples with whom he worked, who seemed strangely insensitive to our peculiar needs and problems . . .

Institutions—total systems—rarely change all of a piece. Change is more customarily introduced gradually, through changes in sub-groups, causing changes in others, causing eventually change of the whole. Lasting change . . . cannot be imposed from without. It can be helped from without by those knowledgeable in problem-solving processes. But the insiders must "own" their change project. They start it. They continue it. They set its rate and its scope.

We had been going at this somewhat naïvely. . . .[1]

## The Institutional Resentment Of Outsiders

We were quite aware that the outside expert has an initial leverage over institutional change that, if he uses it, will produce unrealistic changes, system alterations because of his presence that are not perdurable. I wrote of this as the project began:

The typical experience of an educational consultant is that things change in a school while he is there and that when he leaves they go back the way they were. Things happen while he is there because people give him permission to be different. . . . But typically the *people* don't change, and that is why all returns to a static "normal" when he leaves. The people in the school have the same

1. This is from an edition of Immaculate Heart College's public relations magazine, *On the Move* (September 1971), devoted to accounts of the innovating presently proceeding apace on the campus. Many of these innovations are among those listed by Rogers in his own account of the good effects of the encounter project. (In addition to *Carl Rogers on Encounter Groups*, see his epilogue, "Self-Directed Educational Change in Action" in his *Freedom to Learn* [Columbus, Ohio: Charles E. Merrill, 1969].) But from the perspective of the college report, the encounter project is separated out as an early, disconnected mistake. Everyone agrees that the project was disruptive to academic good order, but some are more bitter about that than others.

capacity the expert has to be different, to be innovative if you will, but they aren't able to assume the permission. . . .

This project . . . is one which wants to see if people in a school can be issued their own "expert licenses"; if they can do for themselves what an outside expert really can't do any better than they; if people *in* a system can feel as free to be creative as the outsider feels by virtue of his reputation, his outsideness, his license.[2]

Though we thus tried to disclaim any substantive expertise—"Look, it's just us plain folks joining you plain folks"—nevertheless we made many members of the Immaculate Heart schools very uncomfortable. In spite of our claims, and in spite of our scientific interests, we were also missionaries bringing a new salvific message. "Try these groups. Mmmm, good."

Insiders have quite enough trouble dealing with their own realities without having eager outsiders who want to bring in more.

What were the realities we brought? For one, a habit of simplicity. We noticed the inscriptions over their doors, we believed them, and in our actions caused them to be exposed as mere slogans. For example, there was the inscription ". . . with a commitment to teaching excellence." And, in our naïveté we said, "Oh, good! And what do you do about sometone who isn't teaching excellently?" We believed in the idea, which turns out to be institutionally very naïve, that you can deal with "problem people" directly, and believing this we made good people of the college uncomfortable, for we were supposing that the inscription about teaching excellence should have immediate behavioral ramifications. An interview I had with a faculty member illustrates the discomfiting challenge we represented in taking their images seriously. The faculty member had mentioned a colleague:

He is very hard on the students. He is so bright that he doesn't understand that they just don't comprehend everything he says at first hearing. And he gets impatient with them.

*Is he a less effective teacher because of that?*

2. "Brief Interim Report," *Educational Innovation Project* (La Jolla, Calif.: Western Behavioral Sciences Institute, 1968), p. 1.

He turns them off. The kids have told me that he doesn't yell at them as much when I'm there, as I have been recently in visiting classes for the interdisciplinary team. Well, I don't know how to say that to him other than—what I said was that I noticed that when he got excited and impatient and his voice got higher, there was a tendency for his students to turn him off. But I don't think I can say, "Some of them have come to me and said you don't yell at them as much when I'm there as when I'm not." I don't think I can say that.

*I don't mean to say that you can or should, but why can't you?*

It would be too hard on him.

*He might get mad. Or do you mean something else: It might really hurt him?*

I don't know. I don't know.

*Do you ever guess that maybe he suspects anyhow that they go to people and talk about him?*

I guess I just don't think about it, about what he thinks.

*The meaning of the encounter for me is that you confront somebody with what you would rather not say because the outcome is entirely problematic. If, instead, you deal with him only in the area of what you're pretty sure will be accepted, that's the kind of leaving someone alone which hurts him.*

Although we said we wanted to be on campus merely to provide occasions for people to talk, inevitably we brought with us our own skills and our own values. They were the skills and values of outsiders who were trained to notice what was being felt but not said and who knew how gently to coax it out; who believed that people on the campus could afford to be more open with one another than they had been—but who would not be around to bear with them the long-run consequences of this openness. The values on which we operated were an embarrassing reminder to many of the faculty of what they were no good at. And we were resented by them, because they believed their *own* experience: that it didn't work very well to be as we urged them—more personal, more open, more direct; and they were doubly tied up for being unable to defend their point of view without sounding cynical, for our operative values were at one with their inscriptions.

There was a certain moral cleanness to our operational attitude about feelings: that it was fairer to confront an individual with how one felt than to sit on those feelings and let them come out later in punitive action or in gossiping. In contrast to the high tone of the educational institution's slogans, the institutional *behavior* pattern was that the professor who turned off his students might never hear how much he was a problem to the college—until the day his contract was not renewed. In the name of not intruding on him or of fostering a healthy diversity of teaching styles, everyone would pretend in his presence that he was not a problem—until the situation had grown intolerable or some way could be found to ease him out. Our wholesome presence was a constant reminder to the faculty of their own derelictions in personal relating, and we were resented for it.

Yes, our wholesome presence. We were even loving. In this, also, we honored not only our own exempt-from-consequences outsiders' values, but also the institution's presentational images. As a Christian institution, Immaculate Heart College gave love an honored position among inscriptions about human values. As a behavioral matter, love could easily offend. One of our research team members told this story:

A colleague and I were to interview two student teachers, both of them nuns, about classroom innovations they were attempting. They lived in the Mother House, next to the college campus, and we made a date to meet them there in the refectory over coffee. They were our friends; we had been in groups together. It was good to see them again and we kissed them in greeting on approaching their table. Not a big kiss, but it was friendly. "You shouldn't have done that," whispered one. "The older nuns are watching, and it puts us all in a very bad light."

We were properly chastened, had our interview, and departed with thanks and a nod. On the way out, passing through the reception hall of the Mother House, we saw hanging conspicuously a beautiful serigraph by Sister Corita. Its headline quoted Chayefsky's *Gideon* and said: "Passion is the very fact of God in man." . . . But don't kiss the nuns.

At the time we thought the incident was amusing and that it simply symbolized the hypocrisy typical in institutional life: fearless slogans high on the wall, fearful behavior immediately beneath. But on reflection, the problem is deeper than that. It is the problem of the ground, which I spoke of in Chapter 11: that one can lose his way who fails to pay attention to the context in which his wishes for himself are acted out. We were affectionate, yes. We were even sanctioned in it by institutional slogans. And when we offended people, we tended to think the feeling of offense exposed *them*. But, on reflection, our affection was a bit unreal, offered as it was without much regard to its context. It was real in a situationally independent sense, real as a virtue carried only from within. It was real in the way the young people have recently been urging us all to be: more spontaneous and a bit regard-less. But it could very well be that institutions are something quite different from that. Maybe good human relations are one thing and passable institutional behavior another. Maybe, in order to survive institutionally, one has to temper his personal wishes, an institution being able to run better, people to stay around longer, if its slogans remain untested, if they are taken as an index merely of high aspirations.

"It's such a rare thing on a women's campus," a student said, "to have men come around who really care, who come up to you and throw their arms around you and give you a big hug and kiss and tell you they are glad to see you. You're a phenomenon." Indeed. Passion—the very fact of God in man. If one thinks of the beautiful serigraph or of Jerry in his encounter group, weeping in the arms of Roz—it's lovely. If one thinks of a college campus, in the light of day, hugs and kisses, "researchers" and "students"—it's ludicrous and embarrassing. The mature person tempers his feelings for the sake of survival, not just selfishly, for by seeing to his longevity within the institution he provides a power base from which to affect society over the long run.

And what of passion? We will make a law, I think: that institutions will gravitate to their lowest common denominator of passion.

But how will the day come alive, without passion? Can one find "an acceptable passion" to offer? No, for passion, by definition, means getting carried away. It is in itself offensive to strict reason. The passionate man might be popular with students—but will have little staying power with his academic colleagues. One risks passion in the faculty lounge at the price of his neck.

When reputable strangers select an institution to scrutinize for science, the residents of that place will be flattered at first and welcome the strangers, but then may quickly feel intruded upon, the more so for soon knowing the strangers as persons like themselves, nothing special after all. This was the more likely considering that the tool we brought to Immaculate Heart, the encounter group, was one in which we would be as known to our experimental subjects as they to us; in which, if faults were among the subjects dicsussed, ours would be as evident and openly examinable as theirs. But we were resented also as one part of a wave of intruders on the college. Immaculate Heart had long possessed a consciousness of its own reputation as special among Catholic institutions, and both fostered this and felt put upon by it. As a special institution, it had been the object of the interest of curious strangers for years. Its weekend experimental Masses, for example, were mobbed by people from the outside community who saw parish life in Cardinal McIntyre's Los Angeles as stultifying and who were eager to leap into the bright and joyful liturgical celebrations at the college. The collegians could not help being both flattered and annoyed at this theft of their privacy.

Since the dispute between the nuns and the cardinal caught the public eye, journalists regularly haunted the campus. The BBC sent a film crew for a week to document this far-out place, this fly in the archbishop's holy oils. "Wonderful," the campus residents said when they heard their fame was to be enhanced—and as quickly, "No, get out of here, all you strangers! Give us back our school!" This was the climate in which we had chosen to study. A student leader told us later:

A lot of people felt that your project was horning in on everything that was going on. A lot of kids say that they felt like guinea pigs, that anything they said would go down on record. They really resented that. At least once a week you'd go into a classroom and there would be somebody from WBSI, and there'd be somebody in support of sensitivity groups, somebody against them, somebody wanting to observe you, the research people from Michigan.[3] I had the same

3. As part of our research design, an experienced team of outside behavioral scientists was contracted to come to the campus periodically to evaluate the change in the climate of self-direction and to try to gauge in objective terms the effect of our encounter project. So, in addition to our own frequent visits for groups and for interviews (hugs and kisses), the residents were being asked to deal with quarterly inquiries by the Michigan people, who had their own persistent questions and research instruments.

feeling on Mary's Day when the television people were filming and observing us. It was *our* school, *our* community, *our* celebration—and they were taking it away!

## The Black Students' Seminar

We were on campus at the time of the growing awareness and acceptance among black people of special racial identity. And in the spring of our first year, there was the tragic assassination of Martin Luther King, Jr.

In a college assembly following the assassination, the predominately white student body and faculty were agonizing over how they might now, finally, be of decisive assistance to the black community. A black student, who had heard enough of superior offers of help for the needy, said, "It's you who need the help, not we!" And following the meeting, she and a group of other black students volunteered to put on a seminar for the college, a seminar dealing with the new black identity and with "white racism at Immaculate Heart." The students proposed the terms of the course and were accepted by the president. Black students would teach the five-week course themselves, the white students learning from their fellows what it was to be black at Immaculate Heart; there would be occasional lectures by black leaders from the community. The seminar's first week would be devoted to group sessions, "in an effort to pinpoint the existence and quality of racial tension on campus."

A large sign-up followed. We were invited by the organizers to attend the first week's meetings, the group sessions in which they would try to build a sense of community among seminar participants, hoping that there would be a willingness to be open, to look honestly at their own racial attitudes and to admit what they saw. "But this is our class," the organizers warned us. They wanted us there to give emotional first aid if necessary, "but don't you do anything unless we tell you. It's our class." We accepted.

The original plan was to have only one week of such group community-building, followed in subsequent weeks by lectures from black experts, lectures on political aspects of black awareness, lectures on existing programs that needed student support, lectures that would aim to see the students got involved with the racial problem beyond the predicted trailing off of remorse about the assassination.

As was our experience earlier in the project, when the immediate success of a first encounter led to requests for more, people liked what happened in the first, encounter-based session of the black seminar. They liked speaking with gentle directness to one another. They liked for a change hearing the evident truth from one another about racial attitudes rather than polite abstractions. So the organizers invited us to come back each week in the future: one session would be lecture now, one would be "sensitivity."

The seminar blew up in the fourth week, on the day that later came to be referred to as "Fatal Thursday." We had been meeting in four small groups, and the experience across groups was mixed, three regarded by participants and leaders as satisfying, honest in not too heavy a fashion, and the fourth as unable to get off the ground. Thus it was decided to have a meeting of the entire seminar, the fifty students and faculty together, to see if the honesty achieved in most of the small groups could be found among us all.

But it was not gentle that day. Heavy, emotional confrontation took place, and I must admit that we played a part in it. The black students had been building up their courage over the month and more of planning and early seminar meetings. They were comfortable now, nearly facile, with the new vocabulary of black assertion: "white racism," "honky," "guns if necessary." This language tended not to be used in the more intimate setting of the small groups, but came out in larger, more impersonal meetings, somewhat in the style of occasional lecturers from the militant black community. On Fatal Thursday one of our facilitators asked a black student about the feeling behind her own rhetoric: "You seem quite personally angry," he noted.

"I am," she said. "I'm furious at you, Sally." She turned to the white girl who had been her roommate. "You say such stupid things! You did it again today. You said"—she mimicked her voice—" 'We must begin with individual relations. We must become involved in each other's activities.' Do you even know? My brother is into the movement and tonight I will sit up with a gun because they are trying to get him. But you were wanting to take me to a party, Sally, stupid Sally. There's no call for parties. You don't even know."

The white girl was in obvious distress. One of our staff asked her what she felt. Tears flooding over the rim of her eyes, she cried out to the black girl, "I didn't mean any harm. I only wanted to be your friend."

Now we were closer to the core of the racial problem at that college, people of good will who worked at cross purposes because they did not know one another's purposes, who offended one another unknowingly and never had heard, who made secret judgments of one another because they couldn't understand the distance that ensued. We were about to get beyond this. But tactically it was a mistake for us to ask for the kind of congruent expression we were getting into, for now there was no holding it back. Students spoke to one another with emotional directness. There were many tears. One student ran from the room and then returned to expressions of concern. The personal hurts had surfaced.

But there was *response*. There was *shared* experience now. There was new realization by the white students of the depth of black injuries and of the fact that they would not be easily fixed over or wished away. On the part of the blacks, there was new awareness that rhetoric was the farthest thing from the need of the movement. By the end of the meeting, there was a palpable intimacy in the air. People were seeing color now, admitting that they saw it, neither letting it traumatize them nor having inclination to brag of how liberated they were, and it was obvious that they could like whom they saw as colored, for no one was holding back any more, no one maneuvering. Afterward in the campus paper, a student catalogued the effect of the seminar: "I've heard things like, 'We've learned to tolerate each other as persons,' 'I've realized coldness is a people thing and not necessarily a sign of prejudice,' 'I think they helped people relate better—they were great for that.' One person even said, 'I've passed the point of seminars.' "

But we blew it. We knew that we had. That night as we returned to La Jolla our staff knew both that we had done what we were good at —had helped people speak to one another genuinely and had provided an occasion for the immediate good feeling that follows—and that we had further damaged our chances of continuing to work on the campus. For now people had an untoward event they could talk about, beyond the ordinary blandness of institutional life. They had been given an easy way of summarizing the seminar, by the heavy feelings revealed on Fatal Thursday. They would have *feelings* about all that feeling, we were sure.

"For some," the student newspaper reported,

the discussion . . . got a little too hot. Some resented "sensitivity session" techniques that led the members of the group to an emotional confrontation with one another—they resented having the group manipulated.[4] Perhaps the presence of the WBSI men did facilitate that confrontation, but I don't know whether or not you could call it manipulation. It is their thing to try and get people to confront the feelings that are operating. . . . If we've discovered anything about race relations, it's that it's a feeling-level thing, and that things that really get to us—the misunderstandings, the slights, the little alienations —cannot be solved by discussing lovely ideas about housing, education and welfare.

But we knew by now who would win this kind of argument. It would be decided that if it had not been for "those La Jolla men," the feelings that were expressed would not have come out. No compliment to our skill would be intended. It would be said that the feelings were not real, that the artificiality of the occasion produced them.

In a sense, we did people a favor. Now they could have the benefit that accrues from emotional honesty, the new clarity of interpersonal vision that gets them beyond the spouting of party lines, and yet disclaim that they needed it. "We do all right on our own, thank you. We have

4. Honestly, all our facilitator said to the girl was, "What are you feeling?"! But that's how sensitive they were: They saw sensitivity tricks everywhere after awhile. One faculty member said to me on another occasion, "What sort of gimmick is that when you look at me?"

no large problems, not messy ones anyway. There isn't one of our problems that can't be solved on a blackboard. So go away, you spill-your-guts guys. And don't hug any students on your way out."

So much for the outsiders.

## On Using The Encounter Groups To Teach Values

A new sense of enthusiasm is one effect of the encounter group upon its participants. When the facilitator style is one of involvement in the group process, as was ours, and when repeated group participation is entailed for the facilitator, then enthusiasm will become one of the notable characteristics of the leader. There will be times when he will forget to pull himself in. With a large staff of facilitators, none of them at the work so long as to have become jaded, our project was bound to suffer the excesses of its own in-house enthusiasts. Our facilitators were experienced, yet occasionally, in their enthusiasm, went after people in their groups. I am sure there were moments when the facilitators were convinced that they knew what was good for others, as they saw what had been good for them: to get better at saying feelings. And, truly, it is impossible not to think it a healthy message to deliver on a college campus, particularly to the faculty. Our own enthusiastic leadership style, then, an enthusiasm that caused us at times to forget that we had no message to deliver at all but only occasions for meeting, was particularly offensive to the faculty. To its credit, the academic mind wants balance, not fervor. To its discredit, it doesn't know what to do with enthusiasm and sometimes sets out to stifle it.[5]

5. A project staff member wrote the following memorandum about enthusiasm and the academy, under the title, "A College Supresses Enthusiasm":

The faculty wants to identify foreign species as quickly as possible. An importation might throw it for a time, but soon it will comprehend the foreigner. If the intruder lies outside the obvious boundaries of the genus intellectus, it will get a clever, depreciating name. Thus, after we were gone, a college bulletin quoted a faculty assessment of our work: "those bleeding hearts techniques."

A college faculty wants to understand one, place one, name one, comprehend one, so as not to see long upset the careful ordering of life which its painfully acquired

To the extent that we trapped ourselves into using our encounter expertise as a vehicle for the teaching of values, we deserved the resistance the appointed teachers of the college mounted against us. We hurt our own cause when we fell into thinking that we knew how people ought to be, and when we used the powerful vehicle of the encounter group to bring them along.

That we were often perceived as attempting to teach values is indicated in the following reaction from a senior college faculty member who attended the first workship and then refused to come back for more.

> The idea seemed to be that we could come to know one another better if we cut away ... anything resembling a "role"—if we forgot that we were [scientists], or sisters, or priests, and talked to each other simply as persons. This may be a valid approach in those cases where being a teacher ... amounts to a nine-to-five job, but I think we have a faculty which is exceptionally dedicated, a faculty to whom teaching in their areas is so utterly a part of their person, that any attempt to separate us from what we are in the college introduces a note of artificiality that to me, at least, is suspect.

This faculty member focuses on a philosophical dispute. But he is also reacting to a personal incident in his first-round group, when the younger member of the facilitator pair, a priest, a man not yet out of graduate school, presumed to show the older man, also a priest, how deficient he was in personal relating. Now he *was* reserved and somewhat stuffy, but he was also well thought of at the college and well

disciplines have provided. One meets this habit at every turn; so pervasive is the resultant onslaught of word games that the newcomer tends to lose courage; he does better to join the game.

With the wit which held sway in the faculty lounge and regulated the friendly distance in their own relations, the IHC faculty members were past masters at assigning clever names to intrusions and so maintaining over the long haul the appearance of imperturbability.

But why, then, was there the reversal of feeling about our team at IHC: from the warmth and enthusiasm of the initial welcome to subsequent sarcastic attack? Precisely because the initial reaction to our work was so enthusiastic. The enthusiasm was something intolerable to the resident intellectual claque and they set to work to suppress it. Had we been smarter, better geared to the intricacies of institutional survival, we would have asked our campus friends, "Please, don't be so enthusiastic. Our reputations can't afford it."

accepted for himself. The differences in personal style between the young priest and the older one were sharp, and the senior resented the presumption of the upstart to make him over. Since he had considerable influence at the college, it was an unfortunate event, politically, that the young facilitator took him on, for this aborted, personal dispute was later made into a key element of purported idealogical conflict, cited as evidence of wide variance between project values and traditional faculty values.

Rogers, senior facilitator in the group at issue, tried unsuccessfully to resolve the personal offense to the faculty member. In a memo to the college faculty, he also tried to deal with the incident on its level as a claim of ideological difference:

> I have been in distress to learn that some faculty members who attended the Montecito workshop for members of the college staff and faculty felt that there was little place for "ideas" in the small encounter groups; that only "feelings" were acceptable.
> . . . All of the facilitators regretted very much if such an impression was created. It is very definitely our aim to permit the groups and the individuals within those groups to utilize the channel of expression which they most desire. If we fall short of achieving that aim, we will appreciate being taken to task by any member of the group. We genuinely wish the experience to be a self-directed one and do not wish to impose any standards or directions on the group.

Yet because we facilitators were in the groups as persons, too, our wish to allow for self-direction among the college staff posed us with a unique dilemma: Clearly the groups should be what the people of the *school* wanted; in that sense, they were not our groups. But we *were* there. We didn't want to be silenced in the groups, just as we didn't want any of the members silenced, didn't want to do nothing, didn't want to with-hold the contribution our own training and commitment prepared us for —didn't want, in a word, to be less than real ourselves. And that meant that often we would look to the *feelings* that were implicit in what these academically minded people were saying. When we did so, we gave damning evidence against ourselves to those faculty who saw all of us as predictable, as (in their expression) always "doing the WBSI thing." We were the feeling fellows.

I suppose they were right, too. But again the dilemma! On Fatal Thursday, the day the Black Seminar blew up, the facilitators were in a bind. The feelings that people were expressing, no matter what the content of their words, were so obvious that we responded to them— and then there was no stopping the sudden flow of further feelings. To have taken the alternative tack and to have responded only to the content would have been to falsify ourselves, would have been, in our view, to pretend that half-statements were the whole truth. One facilitator expressed his dilemma afterward: "What if I were a faculty member at the college? Would I have to resign myself never to hearing meaning, never to speaking meaning openly myself, in order to survive? in order not to be labeled a 'feeling buff'?"

When it was apparent that people meant something quite different from what they said, it was very difficult for us to try not to notice or comment. It is no surprise that there were faculty strongly opposed to our presence. Even when we didn't *say* a philosophy of institutional relationships, we exemplified it. There were times, I am sure, when our relationally skillful presence exposed by contrast the interpersonal deficiencies of many of the long-time faculty. It was like a husband having to compete with his wife's psychiatrist in the matter of empathic listening. Naturally we were resented. "There is room for only one set of masters around here."

It was our irresistable temptation: to see what the faculty were doing wrong and to model for them the correction. Some of the staff wanted to teach demonstration classes for the relationally handicapped faculty. But others on the staff fought to keep our intervention minimal. The former group felt we owed our institutional client success in this encounter experiment; they felt that productive changes in the Immaculate Heart system would not occur without such substantive input. Opposed to this was the stronger feeling among us that once we conceived that our job was to show people how to be or how to relate or how to teach or how to learn, then there would be no end to the necessity of our continuing intervention, no end to the tricks we might think to teach them. The stronger feeling prevailed as the official project philosophy, the notion that our purpose on the campus was only to provide the occasions for people to speak personally to one another. Thus, finally, we wanted no substantive goal of our own for the schools, only a procedural one. But this prevailing view was not adopted without controversy within our own group. A staff memo both summed up our own guru temptation and the cautious view that finally prevailed:

A college faculty member recently wrote that he saw us as being able to help in "the growth of warm and open and human contacts" but was doubtful of our capacity to contribute to genuine innovation on the campus.

His doubt comes, I think, from a confusion as to our purpose: he sees us as somehow offering ourselves to the college as experts in educational and organizational innovation. And, my view at least is that we are not that at all but simply what he admits we are: providers of occasions for openness and warmth. Quite possibly his confusion comes from watching us work. It may be that we forget what we are good at: it may be that we fall into the trap of believing our notices. We do get a lot of personal praise from the members of successful groups, and it may be such praise which leads us into the trap of thinking ourselves great-souled and guru-like. (I can't remember a specific occasion, but I get a lot of praise from my groups at times and I am sure I have imagined a conversation in which someone says, "How can you be so wise for such a young man?")

We err whenever we fall into the trap of being gurus or thinking ourselves expert in anybody else's business. From college faculty members—who surely have their own problems from time to time with omnipotence—we are just liable to get a healthy resistance each time we try to *teach* something—a philosophy of life, a way of speaking, or an organizational theory.

## The Disruptive Potential Of The Nondirective Philosophy

Because of staff vigilance, we were on the whole successful in resisting the self-declared guruship. We fought our temptations assiduously. Our excesses of guruship were early, and we tightened up as the project progressed. There was a change of leadership in the project's second year, Douglas Land taking over the project coordinator's position under the continuing guidance of Rogers. Land was the more cautious to resist the temptations of the moral teacher:

LAND: When are we teaching, when are we leading, when are we allowing for process? There is a point at which we become so sure of the encounter process and where it is going that we then become leaders of the process rather than facilitators.
ROGERS: Yeah. Missionaries.
LAND: Your whole proposal, Carl, pre-sets what we have done. That's the thing about that original proposal, when we know that the best thing for people is to talk openly and honestly. . . .

We were learning that these transparent opportunities of ours for people to speak personally within institutions were in no way innocuous occasions; they were highly upsetting of the status quo. We began with no theory that an institution should be turned upside down; that is just what happened, given our commitment to providing occasions for open personal relating. Ultimately it was our unwillingness to clutter up the encounter with directed interpersonal tasks that defined the disruptive institutional potential of the encounter groups. Without agenda to guide them, participants fell back on speaking to one another as individuals, each from his own feelings. We dealt, thus, with the most persistently potent possible engagement: between persons, direct and unscreened.

The more we struggled within our staff to be nondirective, the more disorderly and disruptive became the institutional impact of our groups. The final institutional rejection of our encounter groups is the more understandable, then, in light of our success in resisting the temptation to lead group members to uniform learnings. That there would be conflict between such a nondirective intervention and the traditional philosophies of institutional management is obvious. "We don't need all these new ideas, all these individual goals," any rational manager would say. "We need loyalty. We need common learning. We need purpose, not chaos."

## CHAPTER 15

# WHAT DID WE LEARN?

Encounter groups don't work in freeing an educational institution. We learned that. You might get by with doing them for a while, but eventually people ask you to stop. The groups are too controversial. They cause explosions of personal, individual growth, people running off in too many directions for the institution to comprehend.

Not only did *we* learn this, but it has proved true in similar experiments elsewhere. Encounter people wear out their welcome very quickly. They are institutionally popular only for the brief time during which their eccentricity hasn't yet fouled institutional functioning. But in short order encounter people are found out as poor cooperators with properly channelled institutional necessities, the groups having spoiled them on a rich diet of direct contact between persons. The whole thing is too much.

## About Institutions

We also learned about institutions. They are different from what people spoiled by encounter might call Honest Human Relationships.

The assumptions on which one acts in an institution are so different from what proves valued in an encounter group that a person conditioned to the one will feel a complete foreigner in the other.

## Is It Good for Business?

Is it good for business? I guess that is the primary question institutions ask. "Business" meaning, for example, Immaculate Heart College, or our tradition, or *The Saturday Evening Post*, or the honor of this country, or God—something that isn't a person and to which, therefore, the individual cannot speak directly. One just has to accept what qualified representatives say about what good business might want of him. As individual human beings themselves, these representatives might sympathize with the sacrifices good business asks its subjects to make. "Listen, I wouldn't want it this way myself. But you know this is bigger than our personal wishes."

One might think it odd that I mention *The Saturday Evening Post*. I got the notion to mention it from an article I read in which Michael M. Mooney, a former *Post* editor, hypothesized that it was when the *Post* became ruled by corporate thinking that it started to go under.

Corporations do not exist in the way that individual human beings do and cannot percieve or act very creatively. But they can grab a notion of what might be advantageous to their backers or to the world—profit being the most obvious example—and then ride it hard, with a single-mindedness that most individuals are unable to muster since they have feelings.

A corporation can ride its idea to death, carrying it on long past the time of its usefulness; and, when it does this, it can cause its members or the rest of the world plenty of trouble. Although the corporation pursuing its aims is as an abstraction pursuing an abstraction, still it can drag individual human persons along with it. The curious thing, since individuals exist and corporations do not, is that individuals often voluntarily subordinate their perceptions and judgment to the corporation's;

curious because when one thinks about it one realizes that corporations really don't *have* perceptions and judgment. No wonder we have trouble!

Anyway, Mooney said,

The failure of the *Post* is not just the story of another magazine going under, but the failure of a style, a system, a regime. In the beginning, the *Post* and its style stood for all the hopes of free enterprise. In the end, the *Post* . . . could no longer understand the new sense of things.

Free enterprise originally meant something a man set out to do, just as Curtis and Lorimer did [in founding the modern *Post*]. But the result of their effort was something called the corporation, and the corporation cannot act as men did when they were free. Corporations . . . are ruled by opportunity.[1]

Instead of *The Saturday Evening Post,* I could have said "The Milwaukee Bucks." In the third year of its franchise, officials of that highly successful professional basketball team spoke of the necessity of a larger municipal arena in which to play their games, since the one the team was using had a capacity of only 10,000 fans and was always sold out. Sports columnist Charles Maher of the *Los Angeles Times* interviewed Bucks' president Ray Patterson:

. . . you might suppose Patterson has been tempted to give Milwaukee an ultimatum: "Build us an arena or kiss us goodbye."

"No," he said, "I don't believe in that approach. I've taken the position that nobody should build a building just for the Bucks. . . . We say they should build an arena only if they think it would be a sound investment and something the community really wants."

At the same time, Patterson said, the people running the club would like it understood they have to do what they think is best for their stockholders.

. . ."If I owned this club with two or three other guys, I'd never think of leaving—the figures on the bottom line are terrific."

But the function of the club, he said, is not to make money for three or four people. It has to be an attractive investment for thousands of people. . . .

If he had to take a guess, Patterson would say the Bucks are not going to get

1. Michael M. Mooney, "The Death of the Post," *Atlantic Monthly,* November 1969, p. 76.

an arena built for them by the city, county, or state. But he said somebody is going to have to make a move eventually. And it could be the Bucks.[2]

Oh yes. This is about as clear a statement of the gulf between personal responsibility and corporate good that one can imagine. Incorporation permits the individual to disclaim responsibility, either by putting off his personal wishes onto the corporation or by suspending his personal good judgment in favor of what he guesses the unmet stockholder might expect. To the average sports fan, the appeal to "the good of the corporation" is frustrating, for the corporation cannot be interviewed, cannot explain itself. If one would interview each of the stockholders individually, he might hear each say, "Individually, I'd like the Bucks to stay in Milwaukee. But it's not up to me."

An institution is at times to be seen as such a corporate body, doing what none of its individual members might admit wanting. If the failure to admit means that incorporation gives members excuse to dissimulate, masking personal wishes in corporate cover, then that is just insidious. If it means that, in backing the corporation, none of the members as individuals truly want what they guess the others want, then it is tragic. It is like a war being fought even if every national leader says—and means—he would personally choose otherwise, "but our country's honor is at stake."

One makes war or moves the Bucks or milks dry the *Post* in the name of and for the sake of the corporation and its abstractions. And no one is responsible!

Only individual human persons can take responsibility. And the appeal to institutional purpose permits them to avoid it.

## Individual Goals and Institutional Goals.

"I think it could correctly be said that the effects of our encounter groups are anti-institutional," Carl Rogers said in a discussion of project

2. Charles Maher, "Bucks and Dollars," *Los Angeles Times*, March 5, 1971, Part III, p. 2.

results. "I think that encounter groups and their outcomes definitely weaken institutional and organizational ties." When encounter groups are attempted institutionally, they turn out to be a subversive influence, for they focus on ends that are opposite from the institution's: they provide the conditions in which participants are likely to act above all else on the basis of their individual perceptions. This proves disruptive to organizations precisely because the institutional need is for coordinated effort. One must suspend his private concerns when mass action is necessary. A war cannot be successfully waged if individual soldiers are honoring their own judgment, reserving to themselves decisions about the veracity of their leadrers. Truth cannot be at issue if there is to be a war, for mass action is necessary in war.

Short of war, one can also see what trouble encounter groups will make with their focus on individuality, private vision, and personal responsibility. Good business demands that corporate members act in predictable manners; but encounter exposure will make individuals' responses less predictable. Each individual, instead of being concerned first for the common good as laid out by leaders, will ask himself, "Is it something I want to do?" That's no way to run a corporation.

## Institution And Encounter

"Do you want to help me with my problem or do you want to tell me something? Do you see *me*—or do you have an ax to grind?" These polarities define the difference that would make encounter groups possible or not within an institution. To hold out the possibility of genuine encounter within an organizational setting, it will be necessary to make it clear that the groups have nothing to do with getting things done.

Is there room for quiet communal celebration within institutional life, occasion for just being together without any eye toward cooperative achievement? If so, this is the occasion in which encounter will fit. But it is not *useful*. It is at most a celebration of the mystery that lies between us.

One of the Immaculate Heart students caught on to this. She said, "If you're talking about a deeply personal encounter group not functioning well, then you've missed the point, because it has no other way to function than for people to be together." We could spend time together. That's all.

In the Immaculate Heart project, encounter groups did not lead to improved working relationships. In fact, they caused some individuals to abandon their work, leaving the institution because they saw themselves as having more possibility elsewhere. The encounter opened them up to the belief that they could have what they wanted—"if not here, elsewhere." Unless an institution is prepared to offer this kind of discovery service for people, a service that could cause it to lose some of its most valued members, then institutional encounter has no place.

A person can be influenced by his encounter experience to speak directly to persons, no longer to institutional necessities. How long he can keep this up in an unchanging institution without being asked to leave or without desiring it himself is problematic. Following encounter, many people slip back to preencounter ways, finding the institutional pressures too severe and persistent to do otherwise. But they slip back with a new awareness that there is more self-responsible behavior available to them. Some decide that it is not worth the expenditure of their energy to fight the system continuously, and they decide not to take the system seriously, to make it a bit of a game. Others simply decide to leave.

People are always for themselves, but there are long periods in institutional life when everyone can forget that, so little is it the appearance. The frequent case is that the truth about the person and his relationship with the institution only comes out when he leaves. He is loyal with his mouth, finally casting dissent with his feet. For long stretches of time, people seem to subordinate their interests to the group's. But experience tells us not to trust that appearance too far, for now and then someone leaves unpredictably. A popular university leader left for a better job. He said, "I must consider the best interests of my family." And everyone nodded. The appeal to family is unarguable. What it means is, "I must do what I see to do." If we protest, still we understand. One takes responsibility for his own life, and we all know it.

If it is strangely gratifying to see a valued organizational person consider his personal intersts and depart the institution, it is because action of this sort can put into perspective the easily spoken words of institutional loyalty.

In the course of my work with encounter groups, particularly with the summer La Jolla Program, which began as a program for campus ministers, I have come in contact with many Catholic priests, whose new corporate habit is to leave their ministry. In his public pronouncements a priest will repeatedly urge his flock to hue more closely to the church's discipline, for he and the church conspire to demand of him a loyal public mouth; and one day, to our surprise, but not really any longer to our surprise, we find him gone—"I can't do this any more." The action can tell us how seriously to have taken his earlier words. In such a case, the early, easy words in support of policy could have misled his hearers in whatever resolution they groped toward in their own struggles between institutional policy and personal inclination. Typically his hearers have had no solid indication of their priest's personal turmoil until the moment they find him gone, and they are right then to feel both betrayed by him and sorry for him; for had he spoken with them of the reality of his life, he might never have had to leave; he might have found the community that is at the base of his search, *but without having to walk away.* When individuals literally belong to a monolithic institution, one often gets his first hint of his colleagues' personal truth only at the moment they leave.

And what if everyone walked away? Well, then these institutions finally would change. But in the meantime we could be led to disaster.

CHAPTER 16

# WHAT CAN WE DO?

Recently, four years after the Immaculate Heart project began, I spent the better part of a day with the original research team, reviewing the effect of our experiment and considering how we would procede differently if we were starting over again. It was no surprise to find the staff in agreement that they would not do such a project again, most assuredly not with the name "encounter groups" ("I'd change the name just as fast as needed to keep ahead of the critics," Rogers said), and not in a weekend, off-in-the woods fashion. They agreed they would want to go a good deal slower than before, working for less dramatic change in communication through existing bodies within the school; they would hope to avoid the establishment of group counterstructure within the institution, one that, while it could attract great initial enthusiasm, would ultimately lead to polarization among school personnel. A staffer said, "It's almost as though the better the encounter groups, and the more excited the participants about their chances for personal growth within the institution, the more likely becomes the early demise of the project." The institution, he predicted, will ultimately belong to its least creative members, those whose lack of hope for personally satisfying lives causes them to be content to manage the spiritual wasteland that the

155

bureaucratic school eventually becomes. People at the top of traditional, large educational institutions have the fun of making the machinery run. Subordinates have settled for fitting into the machinery. Encounter groups are thus a threat to an un-self-confident institutional leadership, for they enliven these subordinate people, causing them not to want to do their routine any more. The groups are thus resisted, the more so for being successful.

A related hypothesis, also a pessimistic one, was :

> The more the school's hopeful people get turned on, the more quickly will they become discouraged, finally to leave, because of the contrast between the excitement of personal engagement with their fellows and the sterility of the enduring bureaucratic process. It is almost to the advantage of the bureaucrats to insure that the encounter intervention succeed, the more quickly will their creative competitors have departed for satisfying lives elsewhere.

If this would go on long enough, the goals of school encounter projects would have been circuitously achieved, most people finally placing themselves outside the established educational institutions, teaching and learning in small communal clusters, the bureaucrats left in charge of empty institutions, no one for them to manage any more—except, of course, the children left behind, who now can be intellectually and spiritually sterilized without interference.

So it won't do to leave.

But what, then, might be done?

## The Institutional Leader As Facilitator

When an outside expert comes into a school, insiders tend, reluctantly or enthusiastically, to yield to his judgment for a time. This is one reason an encounter intervention mounted by outsiders can appear so stunningly to succeed at first—people are talking to one another in the school as they've never talked before, later to feel tricked and resentful.

The danger of too powerful an effect exists to some extent in any functional approach to encounter, where encounter is a fact of life apart from the daily institutional fare, where it is the province of experts or functional specialists. From our experience, we came to believe that this danger would exist whether the expert was an outsider or a psychologically minded insider.

We had long realized in our summer La Jolla Program that in giving institutional people opportunities to facilitate encounter groups, we were not training them to perform a therapeutic function. In the early years of the program there were always a few who came to us with the hope of later setting themselves up in the therapy business, shingle over the door—a quickie course in being a doctor. We were effective in discouraging this sort of thinking. Our brochure explained that "participants are encouraged to apply their learnings to the settings *in which they already find themselves* (rather than establishing themselves somehow as encounter group gurus)" and it expressed our hope that they would use their summer experience only "in the much needed task of making institutional life more personally rewarding to those who are subject to it." When an individual would ask us for some kind of certification following the institute, we would give him our noncertificate:

It is not our wish to certify the professional competence of persons completing our summer program, since what participants later do with their learnings is closely related to their ability to participate as persons in whatever groups they lead, rather than as "professionals," however professionally qualified they may be. There is, of course, no such thing as "certified person," and both the participants and we are reluctant to kid people into thinking that personal involvement in encounter groups—with all the risks to a fixed conception of oneself entailed in truly hearing people and in being gently open—that this can be translated into standardized requirements, technical routines, and professional certification.

. . . We would recommend this individual to you for whatever you and he are able to work out together.

If we were not training people to do psychotherapy, we came to see that we did not wish to train them to perform any function whatsoever.

We wanted to loosen existing functions, not add another. Institutions already are function-ridden; this is one of their major problems, one reason why the encounter had been thought desirable, to get people relating again person-to-person rather than function-to-function.

With the framework of this thinking, we paralleled the main thrust of the Immaculate Heart project with supplemental attempts to tone down encounter by training existing school leaders (a college president, for example, and the entire administrative staff of a junior high school) in facilitative group skills, to be applied in their own existing meetings with the institutional community.

Although, as hoped, this led to considerably less disruption than the outside, encounter intervention, the initial institutional benefit of a principal-facilitator quickly dissipated, for educational leaders typically find themselves spending more time with other educational leaders than in genuine meeting with the people of their school.

Thus a district sent one of its principals to the La Jolla Program, and for a while he was a changed person when he went back to the school. He was more open, more accepting, more community-minded. His meetings were more than announcement sessions. But one of our staff made occasional visits to the school throughout the following fall and reported back his observations on later changes in the principal:

Within a few months he returned to the way in which he was before training. For his primary reinforcement community was not the teachers of his school or the students or the memory of the summer encounter, but fellow male principals in his large district, a group with a fraternal-competitive approach to "my school" and "my teachers" and "my equipment." "You want to know why I've got this great chair?" he asked me as he sank into a chair obviously more plush than a struggling district would allow its principals generally. "I've got a buddy in Central Supply." Within his district's informal fraternity of educational leaders, being a principal was like being a military officer or being a coach. You scrounged what you could, you ran a tight ship, your colleagues kidded you about your success. It was to them that your sense of responsibility attached.

On return to this fraternal reinforcement community, the individual principal who had opened up in training would feel some pressure to make the opening temporary, getting his institution back in control like a good commander or a winning coach, like a principal who might hope to be spotted some day as superintendent material.

To the expectations of such a fraternity, then, the individual school leader typically conforms, rather than to the hopes of his school community. With good reason, too, for the school community rarely meets, and thus, no real community at all, is without influence.

So we learned in this parallel effort that it is simply not enough to provide leaders with new relational skills. They also have to spend considerable time with their people, rather than in the finance committee or with central supply or in public relations work or in shuffling reports and forms—but you know where their reinforcement lies.

The humanizing need within institutional life is not for skills but for occasions. There must be opportunities within institutions for people to meet one another in ways that go beyond the stylized limits of their ordinary functional relating.

## Can The Sense Of Community Just Happen?

"Community is a happening," an institutional critic commented, "and I cannot structure it so that it will happen. It is like friendship. I can hope that friendship will develop; sometimes it will and sometimes it won't. Community happens more when you have common goals; in the pursuit of common goals, sometimes it might happen to two or three in a group of eight; but not to the whole group."

I think he is quite wrong. Community is a fragile enough event that it will not come along very often of its own. Rather, one has to pay attention to it for it to happen. Not that a series of exercises has to be done or a routine developed which later can be called community, but that ample, uncluttered time for community has to be diligently cultivated, for the opportunities will be easy to pass in favor of busy work.

There has to be a certain common self-consciousness for the sense of community to blossom. The self-consciousness that can lead to a heightened sense of community comes when people have the kinds of occasions that imply the permission to say how they feel. Ordinarily there is a conspiracy against this.

Attention has to be paid to building community before it will occur. That seems contrary to what most of us hope about good human relationships. We would rather hope that they would just happen, that they would come along in the course of living, than that we would have to pay attention to them. But the matter of paying attention becomes tolerable when one realizes that it is not that there has to be a technique of building community, but that human events are as worth giving attention to as work events.

There is something very powerful in reflecting together on what is going on among us. Most people who work together do not make this reflection, because of embarrassment or misguided manliness or decorum or self-sacrifice. But as soon as it is attended to, as soon as someone says "Look what is happening among us," then the sense of community magnifies.

We see this in the summer La Jolla Program: that when we get 100 people together in the same room and do not give them something to do, neither to entertain them nor to get them organized, then, in order for community to develop, we have to work at it together. We resist at first; we say, "Nothing is happening here," we say, "This group is too large." But we stick with it, for there is nothing else scheduled, and little by little the community begins to happen. Because, with nothing else to do, yet with the room compellingly rife with feeling, we pay attention. Community can begin when you pay shared attention to shared events, even to the absence of events. If impatience, or embarrassment, or turning out work is the first order of the day, then community will not occur, for community needs attention.

Though we may like each other, a sense of community ordinarily does not begin in organizations with something nice. For the individual, it often begins with an embarrassment that, unlike our usual habit of pretending it didn't happen, can be spoken to the group. In our summer institutes, it sometimes begins when first an individual runs the risk of revealing a little more of himself than he could know in advance would be all right with the group—not by way of confessing something, but often by way of running the risk simply of commenting on a here-and-now issue; e.g., "This is not a good meeting." Because we are known as an encounter-based community, one might know in advance, intellectually, that it would be all right to be open with people; but he could not know it in his feelings, in his fears, in his recollection of experience in the past when he had been turned down for being open in front of people.

A sense of community begins somewhat like an encounter group does. A group leader notes this: "An encounter group is always lousy in the beginning, and you have to wait it out. It won't happen if you go in and say, 'Let's try this for a little while and see if it works,' because if people have the notion that it will be over fairly soon, they can hold out for that time—nobody wants to risk the first honest thing." Community will always begin lumpily. Institutional leaders who always must have things go well from the beginning will not have community, unless their subordinates seize power and find their community in rebellion.

Community is unlike an encounter group also, for community has a note of longevity that typically the encounter group lacks. Because of this longevity, because we know we will likely be together for a long time, personal expression in the community only at times approximates the intensity of the group encounter with its wide-ranging, free-wheeling feeling expression. We have seen that one cannot long live at the pitch generated in encounter groups. But one will have to live occasionally with the honest exchange typical of such groups if he is to feel known to his colleagues.

## On The Necessity Of The Meeting

Since the Immaculate Heart project, I have occasionally been called upon to serve as a school consultant. People who have read Carl Rogers' original article that proposed encounter groups in schools want to try it and sometimes call on me. I have to warn them that it didn't work out very well. If they do encounter groups, I warn, their school might fall apart or they might quit their jobs.

But sometimes they persist and I visit their school. Usually all I can think of to suggest is that the people there meet, that they take time to look around and notice one another. Then I think they will have the best opportunity of doing well by one another and of not regretting their association. Sometimes we sit down to meet while I am there. Usually I do not know what to say, for I cannot guess what is on their minds. So maybe I will say *that*. And sometimes, gradually, if we are lucky, a meeting begins.

I think I do my best work in such circumstances when I can remember that people are bigger than their roles. Sometimes, in a crowded place such as an urban school, it takes an effort of memory indeed to see this, for initially it is not obvious. Often people don't look very meetable institutionally. Kids do, at first, but then they get older, sometimes they get smarter, and their ready, open look goes away.

Sometimes a meeting starts and people in a school look only tired. When you stick with the meeting for a while, say fifteen minutes or so, then they seem angry—teed-off, perhaps, at not having been heard lately and not sure if it's worthwhile to get into it, letting themselves be heard again, only to be dropped again. But finally, because (I think) it is the human tendency to risk being seen and heard after all, in spite of obstacles, if only there is opportunity, finally excitement generates itself, people cluster around one another after the meeting, they talk about what they had been holding back, the annoyances, the jealousies, the hurts—and, yes, the hopes; for community is finally not an expression of complaints but of what a person ordinarily clutches to himself very tightly and brings out of hiding only in community: his hopes. Then it is exciting to be together. Then, once again, it seems that we could make it if we hang in with one another. Then it becomes evident that we really cannot do better anywhere else than here.

Now this is a dangerous activity, this business of meeting one another, unless it is followed up; for sometimes, when the openness begins to burgeon, a person will say more than he has yet decided he wants to say, more than he has decided it is worthwhile to say (for who will hear, really? and if they do, who will do anything positive about it?), more than he has felt it is safe to say, for someone might do something negative about it.

The only solution to this dangerous aspect of meeting with one's colleagues is more meeting: where the regrets at having said too much last time can be spoken of; where if one wants to clobber someone for what he said last time, that too will be spoken of before the clobbering happens. Or at least after. (For there are so many things in institutional life that we *never* talk about communally. Only brood over privately, or discuss in small clusters.)

## Time

To build up close, human, trusting relationships one must have plenty of time, and, often because of our concern for appearances within institutions, such time is what we don't permit ourselves. We are too busy working at looking good. Time is needed, for example, to try to say something that seems true inside oneself and then to say it badly at first or to make a mistake. This can't be a solo performance. To speak personally one needs help. One needs others not to back quickly away.

When such gentle values have not been characteristic of an organization, it is hard for the individual to know how to begin having them.

The larger or more staid the organization, the more difficult it seems.

I can think of two things that may help, and one that will not, when one wants to have a more humane organization:

1. Almost always a special occasion is needed at first if more honesty and trust are to develop institutionally. If one is in charge of the organization, he can call for such occasions with less risk of being thought foolish than if he were not in charge, although there is some risk nonetheless. I am not in charge of very much any more, but sometimes my wife and I are in charge at home. There our call to our children for special occasions has been: "Let us have a time when we can talk about how we are doing together." I have seen this work in classrooms also, though, as in families, having called the meeting you must be careful at first not to use it to present your authoritative version of "how we are doing." You must mean it when you imply that anyone can speak. And if this is believed, the first thing you are liable to hear from others is how you are perceived as a leader.

2. If one is not in charge, then for safety's sake he has to be more tentative when first speaking up. Sometimes making a brief "personal preface" helps. I have heard people who are gifted at deepening the level of conversation do so, not by simply coming out with the honest thing they have wanted to say ("You are a lousy leader!" or "I have always admired you!"), but by first tentatively and gently sating an intention and the dilemma that accompanies it, such as, "I want to talk to you, but I have been afraid," pausing then to make room for the other person. As I suggest this, it sounds like a formula, but it won't work if it is. In order to bring someone to talk to you with feeling, you have to first run the risk of being feelingful yourself. It both works and is the only fair way, because then you locate yourself for the other person—he is not just a target then and you an unknown bowman; he sees you, too, he hears your feeling, and he is not so likely to seem the only foolish person in the room if he responds with feeling. In speaking with feeling, one becomes vulnerable. You must join in this yourself if you want to make it possible for others to do so, too.

3. None of the business of opening up communication in an organiza-

tional setting can be done by rule, because rules promote bluff. I have
witnessed encounter groups, for example, where it is laid down that "We
will only talk about the here-and-now in this group." And then participants start being careful about what they say—they ask themselves, "Am
I doing it right? Is this a here-and-now statement?"—which is the exact
opposite of what such groups are for. Being careful is something we need
less of in institutions. We have too much caution in organizations
already; it is what makes so many of them irrelevant to the times.

The kind of conversational occasions I am suggesting will not provide
immediate solutions to problems, for things have gotten so out of hand
in the competition over running the institutions, the power blocks
screaming at one another, that many disputes are now initially irreconcil-
able; and the only procedure that can be suggested is that the parties
to the dispute meet—not like in a committee or a Paris peace talk, but
where we might come to know to whom it is we are speaking, and what
we ourselves might want to say once the posturing is over. One realizes
that, so often in a dispute, initially one is not knowable. It is difficult
to represent oneself well under pressure, sometimes even difficult to
*know* what might in that moment be a fair representation of oneself.
Thus, in a circumstance of dispute and pressure, the best that can be
suggested is that people take time to meet, and to trust that as persons
come to bear on one another rather than statements bearing, solutions
gradually will emerge.

## An Elemental Event

Meeting with one another is for its own sake and thus is its own
justification. That is one reason it is so easy to neglect. We can most
easily forget to make concrete occasions for those events that ought
always to be going on but that are hard to justify by appealing to some
exterior purpose. Thus a person might say, "Before I die, I want to take
time to think through the purpose of my life." Yet because he has every

day of his life in which to pause and take stock, he can each day put it off, no one day being better than another. He might acknowledge that it is the most important thing he will ever do, but unless he knows in advance the day of his death, other matters seem more immediately pressing. And the time for reflection never comes.

So too with meeting, with taking time to notice who we are with and to hear one another and be heard. Is it important thus to meet, without immediate, explicit, functional, role-related purpose? One can know the answer only when one does it, and between times it will be hard to remember the answer, so basic is the activity itself.

Unless one makes the time (there is no easy way), such meeting of persons will not occur. And then individuals will drift away from their hopes for community. They will climb into their own pockets of self-protective routine. The institution will finally belong only to the few individuals who hold on, who perhaps have the stamina to shape things as they wish, but who finally won't know what to do with their fanchise, for it will have become too exclusive. Everyone else will have spiritually checked out.

If that happens, all over the world (on bad days it seems to be happening), it is hard to think we can survive.

# PART VI
# On Getting Out of the Woods

## CHAPTER 17

# THE ONCE AND FUTURE
# ENCOUNTER GROUP

My friend Weldon Shofstall, to whom this book is dedicated, suggests that the original encounter group was the family. Encounter groups are what families were like when people in families spent time together.

If previous chapters point to the importance of the model of an institution that is small, relatively disorganized, and not well geared for unitary, wordly achievement, that institution already exists in the family. The family is in trouble, of course, but I think it is precisely the experiences that people have gone off to the woods to collect in encounter groups that would help the family right its course. People in families could pay more attention to one another. They could pretend they were strangers. It is conceivable that, if they looked freshly at one another, they might like whom they saw.

One night I met my son Daniel. He is nine years old. We have lived together that long. He will probably be around the house for nine more. By accident we were sitting together on the couch. I was drinking a martini or was in some other way feeling vulnerable. I looked over and saw my son. "Good Lord, that's a person!" It was marvelous to realize. "He could make a difference to me."

## A Potent Tool

The encounter group is such a very potent communications tool that it is hard to find a place that it does not shake apart.

One such obvious place, on the evidence accumulated, is in the practice of psychotherapy. It is a much more powerful instrument than individual psychotherapy, and incomparably more potent than what has gone by the name of group therapy: man in white coat, patients eagerly attentive to his wisdom.

Honestly, the only other institution I can think of where the free, personal, and close communication one finds in the encounter is incontrovertably warranted is the family. People already *are* personal in families; so one cannot say of communication there, as has cogently been said everywhere else encounter has been tried, "This is no place to be personal." One cannot help but be personal in a family. Perhaps that is why so often family members have difficulty being nice to one another over time. People in families are sloppy, unable to maintain the façades that buy them acceptance in the public world.

In all other attempted encounter loci, the very success of the group can lead to a disruption in the participants' other relationships, the ones that exist beyond the walls of the group room and with which the group experience is competitive. If one encounters strangers on a woodsy weekend, then it bothers the people left at home. If one encounters peers in the classroom, then it bothers the fellows in the front office. And eventually all such experiences bother the participants themselves, for they cannot carry them on. Either the experiences are too intensely stimulating to maintain; or participants realize the artificiality of relating so excitingly to these people with whom they do not live, when they continue to be unable to make it at home.

## No Solution

The solution to the problems of human communication will not lie in encounter groups as we have seen them developed, for, with repeated participation, such groups become what one goes off to, away from life. Many of the people who have found themselves slipping into encounter routines eventually stop going to such groups, finally to try to make it with the people already given in their lives, with whom they share the same ground, there to have some of the goods of the group, yet not to get caught up in routines.

Jeanette Hayes went home after the summer encounter institute. She wrote: "At night, each of my children disappears into a little cubicle and I go into mine and close the door. We've done this all our lives. It isn't right. Now I want to pull all the blankets and pillows into the living room so we can sleep together and talk in the dark and hear one another breathe." She was thinking of the twenty-four-hour encounter group she participated in at the program, sleeping bags strewn about the floor, "waking in the dark to a flickering candle and hearing snores from around the room and seeing dark shapes sprawled near me—then rising at dawn, disheveled and warm and looking at the peculiarly vulnerable sleeping ones and smiling at the ones who were awake—being smiled at and feeling so peaceful and close and so belonging and filled with lovingness."

She wanted home to be like an encounter group. It can, though rarely will it be grand. The examples I can muster will rightly be small, the feelings seldom intense, but the effect, I believe, enduring, for at home the people are connected.

## The Family Meeting

When I first got involved in encounter groups and felt their excitement, and saw that they could help me overcome my personal awkwardness, I wanted to be in more. I began to lead encounter groups and I was often gone from home.

Jeannie, my wife, thought that while I was off saving the world, that small part of it assigned to the two of us could be slipping away. So she invented for herself the Family Encounter Group. She said to our seven children, "This will be a regular time when you can talk about whatever you wish." Because they were too young to understand much about "feelings," she explained the purpose of the meetings in terms of problems: "Perhaps you will want to talk about problems you have with one another, or maybe problems at school. You can even talk about problems you have with Daddy and me. I promise we won't punish for what you might say" (thinking that guarantee of immunity might help them get started).

And to me she said, "You can come or not, it's up to you." Because I hated to miss out, I added the family encounter meetings to my list of groups to attend.

At first, as might have been expected, each of the children seemed to see his problems as residing in others. Once Thomas, who was then just a few years old said, "I have five problems,"—and I didn't even know he could count to five—and proceeded to name five of his brothers and sisters. And sometimes they would use the meetings for political purposes: like the time they got together before a session, made a plan, and chose a spokesman, who said, "We don't like the way you always holler at us." And Jeannie said, "What would you prefer?" They thought for a few moments and said, "How about spanking?"

So we tried that—and two days later they called an emergency meeting: "This is not working out very well."

And this week we are back to hollering. . . .

### "Who Will I Talk To?"

But if the meetings were sometimes gripe sessions and on occasion had overtones of political advocacy, still they were surprisingly effective at providing the opportunity we needed to be close to one another, to see one another more clearly and thus to appreciate more deeply whom we saw. One spring, before Jeannie and I left on a vacation trip, David, our oldest, then twelve, said in a family meeting, "I'm going to miss you while you're gone. If I have a problem while you're not here, who will I talk to?" I had to gasp when I thought about that later, because it was all I'd ever wanted in a home: that it be a place where people could talk with one another.

### "But, Daddy, You Never Talk about *Your* Problems"

One night, a few years into our family meetings, one of the children turned to me and said, "You're a pretty good listener, and I can tell you like it when we talk about our problems. But, Daddy, you never talk about *your* problems."

I knew it was true. I am sure I didn't talk about my problems because I was afraid to be vulnerable. It was all right with me when they were vulnerable, I could love them the more, but I could not imagine it allowable in a parent. If I told them some of the things that plagued me, I imagined hearing them say, "Are you not a big person? If you know what your problems are, how come you haven't solved them?"

So I compromised. I talked about some of my problems, the ones that had just come to resolution: "I used to have trouble, you see, getting up early in the morning, but I think I'm getting it whipped now." No help needed. Who's next?

Then one night, I was opening my mouth in a family meeting and an unsolved problem came out, unprepared. I had wanted to be home more than I was, not just coming around for family meetings, but, though I had tried, I had not been able to work it into my schedule. I heard myself say that night, "I feel badly about the fact that I'm not home more."

I could offer no excuse or plan. I was without defenses at that moment and could not explain or account for myself. There was a pause, during which I did not know what might follow, though I could imagine them pointing to the door, "Well, then, get out of here and don't come back!"

But what happened is that Tom, then seven, said, "I feel bad, too, Daddy, but if you have to be gone it's okay. I know you can't help it."

I am home more now. And I think I am home because I discovered in that moment that home is a safe place to be. I discovered that I did not have to wait until I was fixed before I came home, for they knew me already. "Come home, Daddy, we know you're not perfect. Come home and slop around. We all do it."

## Community Defined

I had been searching for a definition of community before that meeting and afterward I was free to write it:

Community means not literally teaching anyone, not literally learning from anyone, but teaching and learning at the same time, all mixed up. It means reciprocal yielding. It means influencing and being influenced at the same moment. It means not always having the right answers, not even having a grip on the best question. It means coming to someone when you are not yet ready to come to him. Community means not deciding everything for yourself. It means letting others have a say in who you are and it means asking them to let you in too.

## Not To Wait

One must not wait for problems, because they creep up with stealth and go past before one can realize it; the deterioration subtly sets in. All the cleverness one can muster is needed to cause the family to meet, cleverness applied to the time dimension of family life. One must make special occasions and must grab whatever further opportunities daily life presents, for otherwise the meeting is put off, to be held tomorrow and never to be held.

We like to travel, and we find that travel presents us with abundant opportunities for meeting. Last year, to escape the spring rain of the redwood forests where we lived on sabbatical, we arranged for a travel magazine to send us to Europe for a month's investigation of family travel.

We flew all night to get to Paris and, mapless, drove all day trying to find the route through Paris to Lyon, to the safety of a French family we knew who had promised us a crash course in the language. We finally settled into a hotel near Paris the first night and found that we could not sleep, for we were too tired.

If one gets the picture of a horrible beginning, he is quite right: nine large and small Americans in a minibus, swinging blindly through a country whose language they did not speak, attacked on all sides by darting French automobiles.

But at three o'clock in the morning, everyone wide awake, someone called a meeting. It turned out that none of us was feeling there yet. This experience, which we had all looked forward to with such excitement, had been yet unable to begin for us. At that moment the habit of the family meeting served us well:

TOM: In Paris, we were just going, and we were passing all this neat stuff.
DAD: Like what?
TOM: Like the Eiffel Tower.
GAIL: And Versailles.
TOM: And all that neat stuff. And now we're heading south to the beaches and we're going to see this stuff we could see in America. I don't mind that, but I want to do some other stuff, too.

So we got out the map and started to look at some of the things we might do, and as we looked, together, I think we began to feel present to our adventure. It was as if we hadn't gotten to France, psychologically, until we announced it to ourselves in meeting.

TOM: Where is the place where there's a lot of castles and stuff?

GAIL: I want to see a castle. Let's buy a castle.

DAD: There's some big cathedrals and lots of castles around.

TOM: Around here? (pointing to map symbol).

DAD: Mm-hmm.

DAN: That's a cathedral.

MOM: I'll bet on the way to Lyon we could take a side trip to see a castle, because we'll have lots of time today.

DAVID: I don't want to go staring, Tom—why do you want to go see stuff so much, like the Eiffel Tower or—

GAIL: I don't want to be like a tourist.

DAVID: All you get to do is stare at it and then leave.

MOM: Yesterday I wasn't particularly interested in seeing sights anyway. And then when we saw that huge building of Versailles, I thought, well, I would like to go in there and see what it's like.

GAIL: I just wanted to see Marie Antoinette's bedroom and that's all.

DAD: David, I think that going to things like that is not good if it's just to stare at it and to be able to say you've done it. But it can be good if it provides us with an experience together, something we can talk about and remember and. . . .

We can interrupt Dad to note that by this point Tom had begun to feel misunderstood. And that is natural, for when one begins to say a feeling, the meaning seldom is made immediately clear. He and his hearers have to kick it around for awhile and react (too quickly, perhaps) before there is room to understand.

TOM: What I'm afraid of is, if we go to a castle and stuff, everyone won't like it but me.

MOM: I'll like it, Tom.

MONICA: I'll like it!

TOM: Because we might go to, you know, sort of a bad one and then everybody will think all the others will be bad ones, too, and they won't want to go anymore. . . .

Tom didn't want people to give up too quickly if they tried his idea. And he didn't want to be blamed if it didn't work out just right. He wanted to be able to say what he thought but not to have it cause him trouble later.

And it seems to me that, in a family, that is a reasonable wish. There is probably no other place where one might hope to be exempt from the consequences of speaking his mind. The family could be the place, the only place unless one goes regularly to psychotherapy, where time is allotted in which one can say what one means with reasonable assurance that one won't get wiped out. It is hard enough to muster the inner courage to speak meaning, without always having to guard against attack from the outside.

## Why Can't It Be Love?

A young theologian said:

It is interesting to me how often people speak of encounter as a religious experience, although rarely do such groups have explicit religious content.

I believe the religious learning in the encounter group is that there is great mystery to be loved in other people, if only we would seize the moments with them. In the stillness of the encounter, one can apprehend the moments as they appear—and then he finds the richness.

At those times, it seems like finding God. Certainly one knows—I know in such a setting—that if you find richness in *me*, I didn't put it here. I have spent my whole life contriving to come across rich. If now, when I am so vulnerable, you find me rich, then that—well, it literally surprises the hell out of me.[1]

Defenses finally down, one often comes through as lovable in the encounter. Others, too; people one thought one never could be attracted to turn out to be lovable in the encounter. A graduate student speaks of such an experience:

During the course of my group I had a most fantastic and rare experience. I experienced an extremely strong attraction to the girl (not much younger than I) who was our group co-facilitator. No words were exchanged, but I felt that there was a strong bond growing between us. When our eyes met it seemed as

1. William Bruce-Douglas, "A Note Concerning Mystery." In W. R. Coulson, *A Sense of Community: That Education Might Be Personal* (Columbus, Ohio: Charles E. Merrill, in press).

though messages—of unknown content—passed between us . . . it was a power-ful experience.

The most powerful thing there is—there ever has been—is the meeting of two human beings. A real meeting, and it can only happen to two at a time.

I guess one of the names that has been used to describe the thing is LOVE. Yet what a difference from what goes by the name of love in the supermarket. Especially the phrase, "I love you," which is bandied about so much in encoun-ter circles.

And yet, what else? Feelings of real warmth and attachment to another human member of the group do occur, tears do come to the eyes, a feeling of confusion hits you. Why *can't* that be love?

One learns in an encounter group that he can love anybody. This realization makes it all the harder when later he sees so little of it in life, when he sees people everywhere failing to connect.

## A Fantasy

There are lonely times on consulting trips when I have been disqui-eted while walking at night through a strange town, by the thought that behind the warm windows of the houses I pass are people who would welcome me if they had an excuse. They would love me if someone would give them permission. I know that if I knocked on the door and said, "I am a friend of your friend in Phoenix who has asked me to call," that would be enough to make me welcome: "Come in, come in!" It would be small excuse, indeed, but I am quite sure it would be all the permission needed for a flow to begin that might come to be love.

But in lieu of the excuse, those people behind their doors keep to themselves the love they could give and I don't do my part, either.

In fantasy, however, though I don't know the people, I walk up to the door, knock, and say, "I don't know anyone in this town. Would you be willing to know me? If you knew me, 1 think you might love me."

In my fantasy, I am also the person who opens the door, and I think, "Yes, I could love you. As a matter of fact, you would like it, to be loved by me. But I can't believe you mean it. I'm afraid to be fooled. What if I said yes and you said, 'Ha! I was only kidding!' "

And so the love doesn't get shared. It needs an excuse, and I understand this, for we are shy indeed, all of us.

It is precisely this sort of excuse that the enounter group has proved to be. We have learned from the encounter experience that anyone can love anyone else, if the conditions are right. And we have learned the conditions. With our typical American skill at achieving the possible, we have proved able to make relationships blossom between strangers, if we can get them into an encounter group.

But although the encounter group is suited to the meeting of strangers, we have yet no easy way first to get them out from behind their doors and not to think they will be attacked. The connection with a mutual friend, as in my fantasy, can provide the necessary permission. But one will rarely be so lucky.

Of course, the connection always exists at home—and it is precisely at home that we are said to do so badly.

Could it possibly be that in sharpening the powerful tool of the encounter, this special occasion that works so well among strangers, we have been preparing for by far the easier and less important case?


## The Reality

There is a fault in my story about the stranger passing the windows at night. The fault is that the life behind the windows is unlikely to be truly inviting; it is rarely as warm as in my loneliness I imagine; the people inside are probably mad at one another or watching television. Thus the first need, to make the fantasy beautiful, is to attend to the life inside, so that there is something truly worth getting in on.

There has to be a love worth sharing that is more than a brief moment among strangers.

## On An Easter Morning

We desperately need contact with the elemental, enduring event, which we cannot think our way around, in order better to know what we want in life. When someone close dies, I think each of us knows better his wish to live the balance of his own life with integrity.

One can wait for the elemental, hoping it catches him before it is too late; he can hope, like Ivan Ilych, to be lucky enough to notice that he is dying before he is dead. Or he can make his own occasions.

The meeting is such an elemental event, but how different from what goes by the name "meeting" in daily, organized life.

Two year ago at Easter we had a long family encounter. We had put off gathering for too long and much was stored up among us.

It was not easy. There were many tears, much to straighten out. One of our number ran out of the room and out of the house and didn't come back for half an hour; but then he came back. And we continued to meet.

Halfway through, there was a knock at the door and one of the children went to answer. Two friends had unexpectedly come to call on us, to pay holiday greetings. And the child who answered the door said, "We are having a family meeting, can you come back?" So the friends left.

It was the most amazing thing, for ordinarily nothing at home is so important as an interruption. We drop what we are doing and say, "How good of you to come." But it was eminently appropriate that Easter morning that callers were sent away, for something elemental was occurring again at home.

Had we lived in an earlier day, when the elemental was more integrated with domestic life, it might have been that someone would have called on the day of a birth. And then it would have been entirely appropriate to send one of the children to the door to say, "Would you come back later, please, a birth occurs." Or if there were a death: "Could you come back later, please, someone is dying here."

It made every sense, as it was, that when the child answered the door, he could say, "Would you come back, please? Now we are meeting one another."

72 73 74 75 10 9 8 7 6 5 4 3 2 1